THE COLOSSEUM

From AD80 to the present day

First published in May 2018

A catalogue record for this book is available from the British Library.

ISBN 978 1 78521 148 5

Library of Congress control no. 2017949629

Published by Haynes Publishing,
Sparkford, Yeovil, Somerset
BA22 7JJ, UK.
Tel: 01963 440635
Int. tel: +44 1963 440635
Website: www.haynes.com

Haynes North America Inc.,
859 Lawrence Drive, Newbury Park,
California 91320, USA.

Printed in Malaysia.

THE COLOSSEUM

From AD80 to the present day

Operations Manual

HISTORY • CONSTRUCTION • GLADIATORS • WORLD HERITAGE ICON

Nigel Rodgers

CONTENTS

INTRODUCTION 6

Timeline 12

1 HISTORY OF THE COLOSSEUM

A landmark of the Roman Empire 18
The Colosseum's zenith 26
Gradual decline and eventual decay 28
The end of the games 30

4 THE GLADIATORS

Training, death, and freedom? 84
Gladiator schools 86
Types of gladiator 92

5 INSIDE THE ARENA

The spectators 106
The ranked seating system 112
Conveniences and amenities 118

2 DESIGN AND CONSTRUCTION

Classical theatres	36
Early amphitheatres	38
Building the Colosseum	48

3 THE GREAT GAMES

Origins of the *munera*	64
The rules of the games	68
Venationes: the morning hunt	70
The noonday spectacle	74
The main event	78

6 COLOSSEUM AFTER EMPIRE

The decline of Rome	124
Quarry, fortress, gardens, bull ring	128
Renaissance revival	132
The artist's romantic ruin	136
The modern era	140

7 THE COLOSSEUM TODAY

Visiting the Colosseum	146
Inside the Colosseum	150
Glossary	152
Index	154

INTRODUCTION

What the Empire State Building is to New York and Big Ben is to London, the Colosseum is to Rome: the most instantly recognisable symbol of the city. But while the other two urban icons are relatively new – Big Ben, the older, dates only to the 1850s – the Colosseum has been the emblem of the Eternal City for nearly 2,000 years. Its antiquity is only one of its remarkable features, however. The great building, enclosed by dramatically repeated tiers of arches and columns, makes an overwhelming visual impact. It has inspired poets, painters, film-makers and others down the ages, from the fall of the Roman Empire to the present. For its brooding, seemingly indestructible mass epitomises both the seductive glamour and the underlying brutality of ancient Rome.

The Colosseum today is the most visited site in Rome. Attracting more than 5 million visitors per year, it is even more popular than the Vatican. But imposing though the Colosseum's surviving facades and labyrinth of elevated arches still look, they are mere husks compared to how the amphitheatre appeared in its prime.

When completed around AD90, both its exterior and interior glittered, very literally, with gold, silver, bronze and marble. All of the 240 arches that made up the three main tiers of the amphitheatre were filled with larger-than-life statues of gods or heroes in bronze or silver, while the topmost circle dazzled passers-by with a row of giant bronze shields. All have since vanished, along with the marble, silver and gold decorations and a great deal of the overall structure. But the great ellipse's ruinous appearance has not in any way dimmed its allure.

Much the tallest building in ancient Rome at about 52m/165ft, the Colosseum's size and grandeur astonished Emperor Constantius II when he visited the city for the first time in AD357. It has carried on astonishing viewers ever since. The French writer Stendhal, visiting Rome almost 200 years ago, summed up the feelings of his age when he wrote: 'It is the most beautiful of ruins; in it breathes all the majesty of ancient Rome.' His enthusiasm and feelings of wonder were echoed by many other international artists and writers, among them Lord Byron, Charles Dickens, Henry James and Mark Twain, who wrote:

> But the monarch of all European ruins, the Coliseum [sic] maintains that reserve and that royal seclusion which is proper to majesty. Weeds and flowers spring from its massy arches and its circling seats, and vines hang their fringes from its lofty walls. An impressive silence broods over the monstrous structure where such multitudes of men and women were wont to assemble in other days. The butterflies have taken the places of the queens of fashion and beauty of eighteen centuries ago, and the lizards sun themselves in the sacred seat of the Emperor. More vividly

than all the written histories, the Coliseum tells the story of Rome's grandeur and Rome's decay.
> Mark Twain, *The Innocents Abroad*, 1869

What all these 19th-century tourists, literary or otherwise, tended to forget in their moonlight reveries around the ruins, however, was that the Colosseum had been built with a very specific purpose: to kill people and animals on a scale almost unrivalled in peace time.

THE KILLING MACHINE OF ROME

During the 350 years that the Colosseum was fully operating, it was the setting for the deaths of an estimated half million human beings and well over one million animals. All were killed for the fleeting amusement of 50,000 spectators. This was done with customary Roman efficiency. Animals from the furthest corners of the empire – the more exotic the beast, the more delighted the audience, rhinos and tigers being special favourites – were transported by sea and land, released into the arena and then slaughtered. In staging gladiatorial and animal games for three-and-a-half centuries after its opening in AD80, the Colosseum was central to Rome's social and economic life.

The Colosseum and its games were a supreme example of the Roman machinery of power, less in a mechanical sense, as Roman technology always remained simple, than in organisational skills. Deep beneath the floor of the arena armies of slaves, assisted by primitive lifts, sweated in the heat and dark of the *hypogeum* (the complex of underground tunnels) to bring up the wild animals for the fights. Far above, 1,000 marines stood ready to unfold the immense *velarium* (the awning that shaded spectators below). And in the arena gladiators entered, fought and exited, dead,

▶ *The northwest side of the Colosseum, the best-preserved part of the amphitheatre that shows the still-extant tiers of arches flanked by columns.*

▲ *Only the western facade of the Colosseum overlooking the Forum still shows the amphitheatre much as it was built. Even here the gilt and marble decorations that once made it glitter have long vanished, making it look more austere than its builders intended.*

◀ *Mark Twain (1835–1910), the American novelist, was more impressed by the Colosseum than by any other building he saw when he visited Italy in 1867. In its noble mass he read the whole 'story of Rome's grandeur and decay', for once suspending his usual criticisms of Italy.*

dying or victorious. Possibly Christians were martyred in the great arena also, although documentary evidence for this is completely lacking. (Despite this lack, Pope Benedict XIV in 1749 declared the arena sanctified by the blood of its Christian martyrs.) All ran with a clockwork precision for centuries, even while the rest of the empire was threatened with collapse.

When the games finally came to an end – gladiatorial contests were banned in AD433 chiefly for religious reasons, although wild beast shows continued for another century – the great amphitheatre lost its raison d'être. It began, very slowly, to decay. This process was accelerated by the tendency to use the Colosseum as a convenient quarry for

dressed stone to build churches and palaces, including the current basilica of St Peter's. The fact that the Colosseum had been massively over-designed enabled it to withstand over a thousand years of nibbling that would have brought a lesser structure crashing down. It also survived earthquakes, lightning strikes and the odd human assault for, among its many later uses, it became for a while a castle.

A PHENOMENAL CONSTRUCTION

The Colosseum is a marvel of ancient engineering. The unknown architect(s) employed Roman architectural principles of the vault and the arch to unprecedented effect. The building is essentially a carefully designed oval honeycomb of superimposed arches and vaulted corridors stacked up for four floors. This is something that today becomes apparent the moment you step inside, so much of the auditorium being a ruin. It is a ruin that now looks rather austere, even stark, but this is certainly not how the Colosseum appeared in its prime.

In those days the audience of around 50,000 Roman citizens entered via their designated arches and, passing smoothly along precise routes, emerged at their allocated seats through *vomitoria,* arches designed to allow the swift and smooth passage of thousands. It has been estimated by modern engineers that the *cavea* (auditorium) was so well

▲ *The Colosseum's operations as a working amphitheatre depended crucially on the hypogeum, the underground maze of tunnels and chambers. Here were the holding cells for wild animals, directly under the arena's wooden floor, which was covered in sand. Winched up from the depths of the hypogeum, the wild beasts, scenery and other special effects thrilled Roman audiences for centuries. (Alamy)*

planned that the entire audience could be evacuated in only 12 minutes.

Far more than most monuments, the Colosseum deserves its unique status as a Wonder of both the ancient and the modern worlds. (Only the pyramids in Egypt survive from among the other Seven Wonders of the Ancient World, and they cannot be approached so closely or entered so easily as the Colosseum.) Yet there is an ambivalence in modern attitudes to the great amphitheatre. Everyone can admire its architectural and engineering brilliance, saluting the Roman genius at so swiftly erecting enduring yet immensely practical buildings.

All this technical brilliance, however, was aimed solely at facilitating the viewing of mass slaughter of human beings and wild animals. Unlike the Pantheon, or parts of the Baths of Diocletian, the Colosseum could not really

◄ *The Colosseum at night, as seen from the Forum Romanum. Modern lighting has made it possible to illuminate the amphitheatre far more dramatically than the ancient Romans could when the building was actually in use. This makes up for the disappearance of the flamboyant gilt and silver statues that once filled every arch.*

be turned into a church. Nor could it be converted into an almost impregnable fortress, as happened with the Castel Sant'Angelo, which was originally a mausoleum for the family of the emperor Hadrian. The memory of bloodshed and mass executions– whether of Christian martyrs or others condemned as criminals – sometimes still hang over the great arena. It forms a central part of the mingled glamour and brutality of ancient Rome, which simultaneously fascinates and repels. While the Egyptian pyramids were built by a people who seem unimaginably distant from us, and the Parthenon in Athens was erected by a city fired by what now seem impossibly high ideals, the Colosseum was unashamedly built as a crowd pleaser, providing popular free entertainment. It still today pleases the crowds, attracting more than five million visitors a year, so making it one of the world's top tourist attractions.

THE PARAGON OF AMPHITHEATRES

The Colosseum could be called the mother of amphitheatres. While it was certainly not the first stone amphitheatre to be built in the Roman Empire, it soon became the archetypal arena and was copied around the empire. From Arles in southern France to Djema in Tunisia, imitators great and small sprang up. All paid their respects to the great Roman arena by emulating its tiers of arches. None, however, competed with it in terms of size and luxury.

The Colosseum is also the ancestor of much more recent places of mass public entertainment, whether they are sports stadia or opera houses. The Astrodome in Houston, one of the largest of all sports stadia, owes its creation in 1965 to Roy Hofheinz, once mayor of Houston, who had been hugely impressed by seeing the Colosseum. The vast enclosed stadium was even about the same size as the Roman arena, seating about 50,000 people, but it is now no longer used for sporting events due to new safety regulations. London's Coliseum, a music hall turned opera house, dates from 1904 and is still in use, by contrast. Its architect Frank Matcham designed it with a panache and lavishness that deliberately recalled the ornate splendours of the first building to bear that name. Seating only about 2,500, however, it is much smaller than either the Roman or the Texan buildings.

The half-ruined great amphitheatre in the centre of Rome remains the paradigm against which all such later buildings are measured. This book outlines the Colosseum's long and surprisingly varied history, explains its purpose – which was as much to do with politics as entertainment – details its technical operations and describes the varied games that took place within it. Finally, it suggests the best times and ways to visit one of the world's most popular monuments.

COLOSSEUM TIMELINE

BC

c500 First murals depicting gladiatorial games in Campania; in Rome, new Republic established after expulsion of the last Etruscan king Tarquinius Superbus. Senate, composed of noblemen, becomes dominant force in state

264 First recorded gladiatorial games in Rome. Start of First Punic War with Carthage (until 241)

218 Start of Second Punic War (until 202)

216 Hannibal, Carthaginian general, defeats Roman armies at Cannae, Rome's worst military disaster of the Second Punic War

215 Games given in honour of Aemilius Lepidus, Roman nobleman, involve 22 pairs of gladiators in Forum Romanum, an act defying Hannibal's threat

202 Battle of Zama: Hannibal's defeat and end of Second Punic War; Rome occupies much of Spain

200–196 Second Macedonian War gives Rome indirect control of Greece

174 Quintus Flaminius, conqueror of Greece, gives *munera* in honour of his father in Forum Romanum with 74 pairs of men fighting each other

169 First known *venatio*, animal hunt involving 63 leopards, 40 bears and some elephants held in the Circus Maximus

167 Sack of Epirus, western Greece, brings 150,000 Greek slaves to Rome

146 Sack of the wealthy cities Carthage and Corinth: Greece and North Africa become Roman provinces. Rome effective ruler of the whole Mediterranean

73–71 Revolt of gladiators led by Spartacus spreads across Italy and threatens Rome itself; initially successful but finally defeated by Crassus, multi-millionaire and aspiring politician

70 Amphitheatre built at Pompeii for a colony of retired legionaries, the first all-masonry amphitheatre in Italy

65	Julius Caesar (right), aspiring politician, gives unprecedentedly lavish games with 640 gladiators in Rome in Forum. Senate, alarmed by his ambition, passes laws to restrict size of games
60	First Triumvirate, secret cabal, formed of Caesar, Crassus and Pompey, a successful general and aspiring politician
61–55	Building of the Theatre of Pompey, Rome's first permanent masonry theatre
58–51	Caesar's conquest of Gaul (France)
59	Quintus Cicero, brother of the orator Marcus and governor of Roman province of Asia, complains of difficulty in finding enough wild animals for the arena
50	Caius Scribonius Curio, aspiring politician, builds Rome's first double theatre or 'amphitheatre', a temporary wooden structure in two moving sections
46	Caesar, now dictator of Rome, gives games that include *naumachia,* mock naval battles involving 6,000 gladiator-sailors to celebrate his triumphs in Gaul and the East in specially constructed stadium by the Tiber
44	Caesar's assassination by Republicans led by Marcus Brutus sparks new round of civil wars
42	Republicans defeated at Battle of Philippi: Octavian takes western half of empire, Mark Antony the eastern
31	Battle of Actium: Octavian, Caesar's adopted son, defeats rival Mark Antony to become undisputed master of reunited Roman Empire, annexing Egypt
29	Taurus, one of Octavian's finest generals, builds first permanent small amphitheatre in Rome
27	Octavian adopts name Augustus, effectively establishing new monarchy
13–11	Building of Theatre of Marcellus (right), stylistic forerunner of Colosseum, by Augustus in honour of his recently deceased son-in-law Marcellus

AD

14	Death of Augustus; succeeded as emperor by Tiberius
37	Death of Tiberius; accession of Gaius Caligula, keen follower of the *munera*
41	Caligula assassinated; Claudius becomes emperor
50–53	Building of Amphitheatre of Verona, largest stone-built amphitheatre in Italy to date, in 'Italian' style
52	Claudius gives *naumachia* on Fucine Lake near Rome that ends in shambles
54	Death of Claudius; Nero becomes emperor
57	Nero orders construction of Rome's largest wooden amphitheatre. Lavishly decorated, it dazzles onlookers and reputedly seats 50,000 spectators
59	Riots at amphitheatre of Pompeii lead to ban on games there for ten years

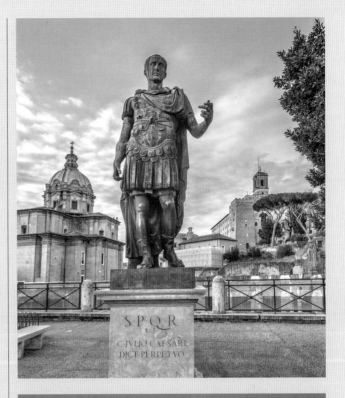

64	Great Fire lays waste most of Rome, including amphitheatre of Taurus and that built by Nero; Nero seizes chance to build his vast *Domus Aurea* (Golden Palace), above, with huge statue of himself as the Sun God outside, nicknamed the Colossus. Christians burned as scapegoats for the fire in the Circus Maximus
66	Revolt of Jews in Judaea (Israel/Palestine); Vespasian appointed to command Roman army in the East; Josephus, Jewish general, changes sides
68	Overthrow of Nero: civil war and the 'Year of the Four Emperors'
69	Vespasian wins civil war and becomes sole emperor
70	Sack of Jerusalem by Titus, Vespasian's son, effectively ends Jewish revolt; spoils from the Temple (above) go towards building Colosseum
*c*72	Start of construction of Colosseum on site of the drained lake of the *Domus Aurea*. Named *Amphitheatrum Flavium after* the new Flavian dynasty
79	Death of Vespasian, accession of Titus; eruption of Vesuvius destroys the cities of Pompeii (bottom left) and Herculaneum
80	Grand inaugural games involving 5,000 animals, about 3,000 men and a *naumachia* over 100 days open the Colosseum; the poet Martial praises the Colosseum and the Flavian dynasty in his *Liber Spectaculorum* (Book of the Games)
81	Death of Titus; accession of his brother Domitian
*c*85	Last *naumachia* held in Colosseum; start of construction of *hypogeum* beneath arena floor and completion of topmost floor of Colosseum
*c*90	Start of construction of Ludus Magnus, the main training school, completed under Hadrian
96	Assassination of Domitian; Nerva, elderly senator, becomes emperor and adopts young general Trajan as his heir
98	Trajan succeeds Nerva as emperor
101–106	Dacian Wars lead to conquest of Dacia (Romania)
108	Trajan celebrates his Dacian triumph with games of unprecedented splendour, with 10,000 war captives and 11,000 wild animals fighting in the arena
*c*120	Ludus Magnus completed
146	Lightning damages the Colosseum
168	Marcus Aurelius, emperor since 161, enlists gladiators in army to fight sudden German invasion

180	Commodus succeeds Marcus Aurelius as emperor and becomes enthusiastic amateur gladiator
192	Commodus stages elaborate games in the Colosseum with himself as chief protagonist. He is assassinated soon after
193	Septimius Severus becomes emperor during renewed civil wars
200	Septimius bans women gladiators
217	Lightning strike sparks major conflagration. Colosseum closed for repairs
222	Ceremonial reopening of the Colosseum under emperor Alexander Severus, although much remains to be repaired
235	Assassination of Alexander; beginning of the 'years of anarchy', with empire torn apart by recurrent civil wars and foreign invasions
248	Emperor Philip the Arab celebrates Rome's millennium with lavish games in the Colosseum
260	Emperor Valerian captured by Persians (top right); his son Gallienus becomes emperor but proves unable to prevent many eastern and western provinces from breaking away
262	Colosseum shaken by major earthquake in Rome
274	Emperor Aurelian celebrates reunion of empire with major games in Colosseum
284	Diocletian becomes emperor and starts reorganising empire into Tetrarchy: four rulers system, two emperors in the West and two in the East, all ruling from new administrative capitals near the frontiers such as Milan or Trier
303–311	Last and greatest official persecution of Christians
306	Constantius I, senior emperor in West, dies in York; succeeded by his son Constantine I, who at first only rules westernmost provinces
312	Constantine becomes sole ruler of Western Empire after defeating Maxentius at the Battle of the Milvian Bridge outside Rome. Converts to Christianity
313	Constantine and Licinius, emperor in the East, issue Edict of Milan, offering tolerance to all religions
324	Constantine defeats Licinius to become sole emperor; bans courts from condemning criminals to the arena, makes Christianity officially favoured state religion
330	Constantine founds Constantinople (today Istanbul), a new Christian capital on the Bosphorus. No amphitheatres built in the 'New Rome'
357	Emperor Constantius II is awestruck by Colosseum on visit to Rome but gives no *munera*
391	Emperor Theodosius I's official ban on public pagan worship a blow to the games, still closely linked to the old rites
392	Roman aristocrat Symmachus's attempt to stage games proves a fiasco
395	Empire divided between sons of Theodosius, Honorius in the West and Arcadius in the East, never to be reunited

405	Monk Telemachus leaps into arena to separate combatants. He is killed and soon seen as martyr. Honorius ineffectually tries to ban games
410	Visigoths sack Rome but move on
429	Earthquake damages amphitheatre's top floor, probably starting building's decay
c433	Last *munera* held in Colosseum but *venationes* still sometimes staged
455	Vandals sack Rome, looting it rapaciously
476	Deposition of boy-emperor Romulus Augustulus by German mercenaries signals final end of Roman Empire in the West
c535	Last *venationes* staged in Colosseum

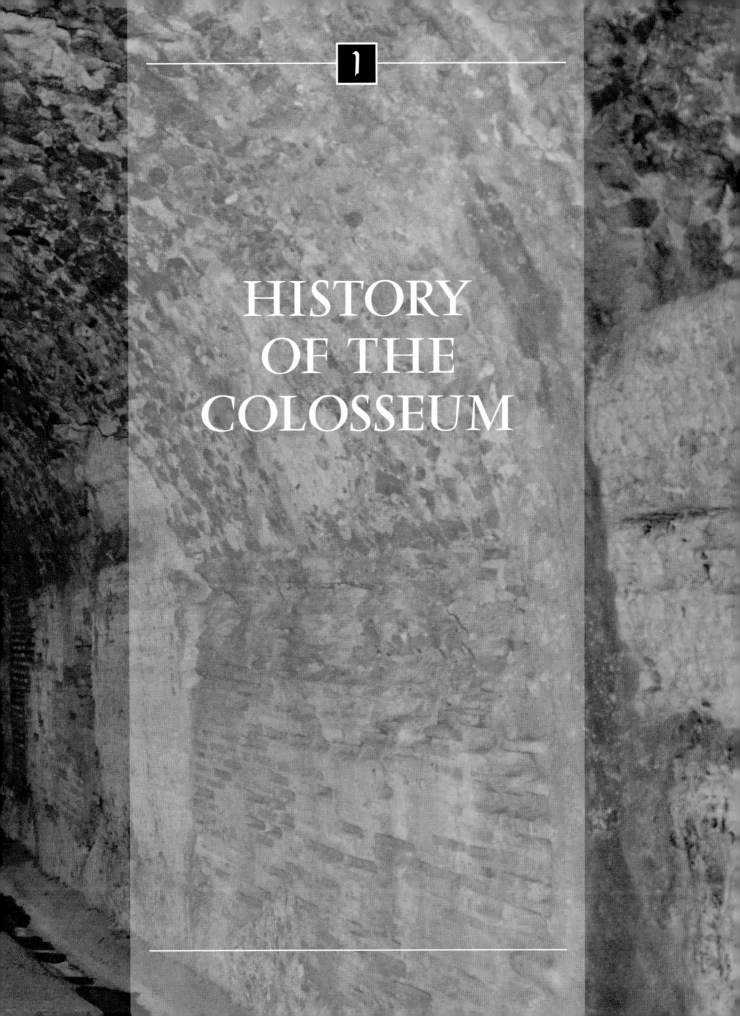

1

HISTORY
OF THE
COLOSSEUM

A LANDMARK OF THE ROMAN EMPIRE

The Colosseum, the most famous of all arenas in the world, owes its creation at least in part to Roman civil war. In the summer of AD70 Rome had celebrated the arrival of a new emperor, Vespasian. This was hardly a novelty for the city by then. In the previous two years of civil wars the city had seen four Roman emperors acclaimed and then deposed. Vespasian, however, proved to be there to stay. He founded a new dynasty, the Flavian, and he commissioned what soon became Rome's most celebrated building.

The Flavian Amphitheatre – its original name, Colosseum being a later nickname that stuck – *was* a novelty in Rome. The city, despite being the largest in the world, had had no permanent large-scale amphitheatre before then. Instead gladiatorial games had been held at several temporary sites, including the Forum Romanum, which was the square at the centre of Rome's life, in the Circus Maximus – which dated back to the 6th century BC – and in temporary wooden amphitheatres.

This was a strange lack. The amphitheatre was where the emperors confronted and entertained the Roman people and

▶ *The Colosseum as seen from the west, showing that much of the building no longer preserves its original four-tiered aspect due to centuries of depredation.*

▼ The Circus Maximus *by Jean-Léon Gerôme, a dramatic yet accurate depiction. Larger than the Colosseum, the Circus seated around 300,000.* (Getty)

▲ *The amphitheatre at Pompeii, in the shadow of Mount Vesuvius, dates from around 70BC and was the first permanent masonry amphitheatre erected in Italy.*

were hailed – or booed – by them in turn, and where Rome's brutal justice was meted out to criminals and outcasts. One reason for the lack of permanent amphitheatres inside Rome was government fear of public disorder. Rivalry between people from Pompeii and the nearby town Nuceria after games in AD59 had caused full-scale rioting in Pompeii's permanent amphitheatre, leading to a ban on games there for ten years. There was also an element of religious puritanism. Erecting permanent structures solely for entertainment inside the city's *pomerium* (sacred boundary) was thought profane by old-fashioned Romans, who were very religiously minded.

WOODEN AMPHITHEATRES: LARGE, LUXURIOUS, FLAMMABLE

Some of Rome's temporary wooden amphitheatres had been most impressive structures. That commissioned by the emperor Nero in AD57, for example, was so flashily decorated in marble and gilt that onlookers were reputedly dazzled by its brilliance. It may have seated about 50,000 people – a very good size – but it was destroyed in the Great Fire that laid waste three quarters of the city in AD64. There was also an amphitheatre built partly in stone, partly in wood in 29BC by Taurus, a successful general under the emperor Augustus. It became too small though for the increasingly grandiose entertainments put on by the emperors. The emperor Gaius Caligula (reigned AD37–41) spurned it for just such reasons.

Taurus's amphitheatre also burnt down in the Great Fire, leaving no traces.

NERO'S GOLDEN PALACE

Nero's real architectural achievement had been his Domus Aurea (Golden Palace), a huge complex of palaces and parkland that reputedly occupied 120ha/300 acres in the heart of Rome. It boasted a revolving dining room that sprayed perfume on to guests, elaborate frescoes and a lake. It was regarded as shockingly sybaritic by most Romans.

Just outside the palace complex stood the huge gilded bronze statue 30m/97ft high that was called the Colossus, recalling a similar statue of the Sun God in Rhodes. (Its name later was given to the amphitheatre too.) The statue depicted Nero standing naked, his head ringed by sunbursts, so identifying himself with the Sun God. This very Greek concept shocked many Romans, not least because of its nudity – the Romans preferred their emperors to appear suitably dressed. Nero, increasingly narcissistic, was unconcerned by popular disapproval. When the palace was completed, he exclaimed: 'Now at last I can live like a human being!' He did not live like one for long, being overthrown soon after.

Nero, the last of the Julio-Claudian dynasty, descended from the great Julius Caesar himself, finally alienated all of Rome by his extravagance, megalomania and neglect of official duties. Vespasian, in contrast, came from a minor provincial Italian family. He had been a successful general, renowned for his skills in capturing British hill forts, and then had a successful civilian career as a senator and consul in Rome in the normal Roman pattern. But he had not proved a good courtier, once

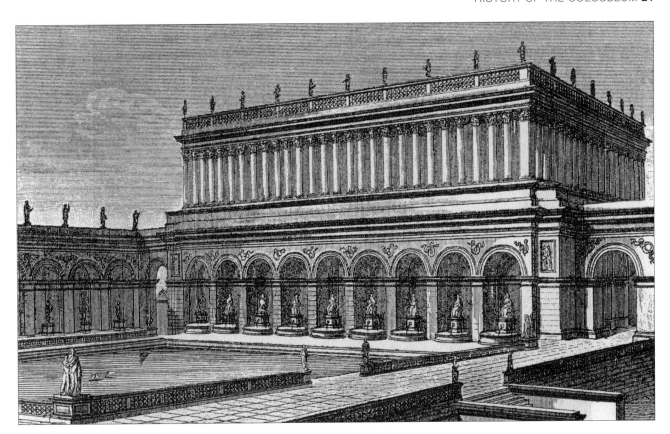

▲ *Nero's Domus Aurea (Golden Palace) took up 120ha/300 acres of prime real estate. Only five years later it was mostly demolished to make way for the Colosseum. (Mary Evans)*

▶ *The Colossus of Rhodes was a gigantic statue of Helios the sun god that reputedly bestrode the entrance to Rhodes Harbour. Nero ordered the erection of a similar statue, bearing his own features and also called Colossus, outside his new palace. (Getty)*

▲ *A corridor inside the ruins of the Domus Aurea, Nero's Golden Palace, which is now wholly underground. It was in its time very unpopular with the citizens of Rome.*

▲ *Emperor Vespasian began the construction of the new amphitheatre in Rome. He was a rugged, old-fashioned soldier who knew how to please the people.*

falling asleep during one of Nero's lengthy poetry recitals (the emperor thought himself a great performance artist). For this lapse Vespasian was banished from Rome in disgrace.

A revolt in Judaea (modern-day Israel/Palestine) in AD66 led to his recall, however, and he was given command of the armies in the east. Vespasian was systematically crushing the Jews – divided and untrained they seldom proved a match for Rome's disciplined legions – when news came of Nero's fall in AD68. Leaving his elder son Titus to deal with the Jewish revolt, Vespasian joined the imperial contest at exactly the right moment. By the summer of AD70 he was universally accepted as emperor.

VESPASIAN'S COLOSSAL UNDERTAKING

Aged 60 at the time of his accession, Vespasian was a plain-speaking old-fashioned Roman with a rustic sense of humour. Unlike his predecessor, Greek art and luxury had no appeal for him but he did see the need to impress the Roman people with a grand gesture. So, on the site of Nero's private park he ordered the erection of a building for the whole people: a giant amphitheatre to stage the most popular of Roman entertainments, gladiatorial games. Although known initially as the Flavian Amphitheatre, it well deserves its later name, Colosseum. Building it was to prove a colossal undertaking.

Vespasian and his architects – whose names remain unknown, unlike those of the architects for some earlier and

A DOUBLED-UP THEATRE

Pliny the Elder (AD23–79), an encyclopedic and prolific author, described a strange forerunner of the Colosseum. It was built in 50BC by Caius Scribonius Curio. Curio was a politician obviously trying hard to impress the electorate, when Rome was still a Republic and not the dictatorship it was soon to become. The building consisted of two wooden semi-circular theatres revolving on pivots.

'He [Curio] built close to each other two very large wooden theatres, each poised and balancing on a revolving pivot. In the morning a play was performed in each of them and they faced in opposite directions, so that the actors in each would not drown out the other cast's words. Suddenly the theatres revolved – it seems that after the first few days they did so with some spectators actually staying in their seats – the corners of the two theatres met, and Curio created an amphitheatre in which to stage gladiatorial fights.'

Slaves must have provided most of the muscle power behind this remarkable transformation but neither Roman technology nor Roman sang-froid should be underestimated.

later buildings – chose a place that at first sight might seem odd: the lake of Nero's palace. But there were good reasons behind their choice. When drained, the lake proved to have firm clay soil beneath it. This was vitally important because the Colosseum was among the most massive and weighty edifices the Romans ever built. (Although later public baths such as those of Caracalla and Diocletian, both erected during the 3rd century AD, were larger in area, they were much lighter structurally with their soaring domes and arches.)

Further, the lake would have had water channels, pipes and drains to fill and empty it. This was essential for the new amphitheatre, as almost certainly it was initially intended to host *naumachia* (mock naval fights) as well as land contests.

THE GRAND INAUGURATION

Vespasian died in AD79, before the completion of the greatest building of his dynasty. It was left to his elder son and successor Titus to inaugurate the grand new amphitheatre.

Titus opened the Colosseum in AD80 with games of unparalleled munificence that lasted for three months, although games were not held every day. During this time, over 9,000 wild animals were killed – among them lions, leopards, tigers, wild boars and bulls. Female hunters killed some of these, one of the rare instances when women are definitely known to have appeared in the great arena. And

thousands of pairs of (male) gladiators fought each other. However, most of these trained performers, who were more expensive to procure and train even than exotic wild beasts, would have survived to fight again.

Titus's games also seem to have included *naumachia*, the mock naval battles for which the arena must have been flooded. The poet Martial (AD40–104) praised these performances so sycophantically in his *Liber Spectaculorum* ('The Book of the Games') that he is known as the Flavian dynasty's poet laureate. Unfortunately, Martial tends to be long on hyperbole and short on solid detail:

> Here, near where adorned with stars the Colossus (statue of Nero)
> Gazes up at heaven, once gleamed the palace of a brutal ruler Overshadowing the city. Here where the mass of the Amphitheatre now rises nobly up, was once Nero's lake. Here where we now admire warm Public baths, a palace once robbed poor people of their homes.
>
> A contemporary view from Martial, *Liber Spectaculorum* ('The Book of the Games')

▼ *In this model of ancient Rome in the Museo della Civiltà Romana, the Colosseum (top right) can be seen looming over all other buildings. (Getty)*

▲ *The ruins of the vast palace built by the emperor Domitian on the Palatine Hill – our own word 'palace' derives from it.*

◄ *The Arch of Titus, erected by Domitian in memory of his elder brother Titus near the west side of the Colosseum.*

DOMITIAN AND THE FINAL TOUCHES

Titus, who liked to be seen as generous to his friends but ruthless to his enemies – he had brutally put down risings in Britain before going on to crush the revolt in Judaea, showing no mercy in either province – died suddenly in AD81. He was widely and genuinely mourned. Power then passed to his younger brother Domitian, a far less likeable character whose growing paranoia and erratic behaviour ultimately led to his assassination. However, Domitian energetically continued the Flavian family's building programme. He erected the Meta Sudans – a grand fountain near the amphitheatre – a triumphal arch in memory of his elder brother just to the west of the Colosseum (The Arch of Titus), and an immense new palace on the Palatine Hill rising above it, which became the main imperial residence until the fall of the empire. (The English word 'palace' comes from Palatine.)

During Domitian's reign (AD81–96) the Colosseum gained its top fourth floor and its final impressive form. The amphitheatre's elliptical outer circle measured 188m/610ft by 156m/510ft, and when it was wholly intact rose to about 52m/169ft. This made it the tallest building in all Rome, even ignoring the tall poles that held aloft the *velarium, ie* the huge retractable sunshade that rose above the amphitheatre itself. The amphitheatre now probably gained its final external form, with marble or painted stucco covering its brick, concrete and stone structure, larger-than-life statues of heroes and gods filling the arches and gilded bronze shields lining the uppermost circle. When intact, it must have gleamed resplendently. This glitter, which so appealed to Romans, is hard to visualise today when we have only the amphitheatre's bare skeleton to admire.

In the Colosseum Domitian staged numerous games of suitable extravagance. He also tried holding Greek-style athletic contests that did not involve bloodshed in the arena, probably for reasons of economy rather than humanity. These bloodless events never proved popular with the Roman people, however, who were addicted to their brutal thrills.

Under Domitian the Colosseum must have lost its amphibious capability, meaning that it could no longer stage naval combats. Roman sources are unclear as to how the arena itself had been initially flooded but the amphitheatre now certainly gained a proper *hypogeum*, the complex subterranean system of lifts, trapdoors, pulleys, passages and cells essential to the staging of the great games. This would have prevented further *naumachia*, as it must have been impossible to waterproof effectively the machinery in the lower parts of the arena. Instead, *naumachia* were from now on held in specially built arenas near the river Tiber, where water in copious amounts was more freely available.

TITUS AND THE JEWS

Prominently sculpted on the Arch of Titus – which was started by Titus himself but probably finished by his brother – to the west of the Colosseum is Titus's triumphal procession of AD70 in Rome. Titus had just ended the main Jewish revolt in Judaea by capturing Jerusalem. The whole of Jerusalem's population was killed or enslaved and the city itself almost completely destroyed. Just two towers and some walls were left standing. The Jews must have felt they were the special targets of Roman vengeance. The flaunting of the Menorah, taken from the Temple of Jerusalem – clearly shown on the arch – caused particular outrage and is still remembered. To this day many Jewish people prefer not to walk under the Arch of Titus. Certainly *manubia* (plunder from Jerusalem) paid for part of the cost of the amphitheatre and Jewish captives were among the slave labourers who helped build it.

To regard Titus or other Romans as being anti-Semitic in a modern sense would, however, be a mistake. The Romans used exemplary brutality to discourage all revolts. They had earlier destroyed Corinth and Carthage, both important and wealthy cities, in exactly the same way, their actions being motivated not by racism but realpolitik. After the war Titus took as a mistress the Jewish queen Berenice, who had prudently left Judaea before the revolt. He also had a protégé in Josephus, a turncoat Jewish general who had joined the Romans rather than commit suicide when defeated. Josephus later wrote a colourful if unreliable history of the wars, praising himself and disparaging other Jewish leaders. Many Jews were living peacefully around the multiracial empire – in Egypt, Syria, Greece and Italy – well before the revolt of AD66.

▼ *Detail from the Arch of Titus showing the Menorah, the seven-branched candlestick looted from the Temple of Jerusalem by Roman troops.*

THE COLOSSEUM'S ZENITH

During the Colosseum's glory days the amphitheatre was a metaphor of the complex relationship between a Roman emperor and the people. Romans had high expectations when it came to public entertainment, and emperors accepted that part of their success was in the hands of the common people.

IMPERIAL OBLIGATIONS

In the reign of Trajan (AD98–117) the Roman Empire reached its widest extent. It now stretched from southern Scotland to the Persian Gulf. Greatest of Trajan's conquests was Dacia (modern Romania), a land then rich in gold. To celebrate this victory, Trajan held games in AD108–109. The games involved 11,000 wild animals, which would have almost all died in the *venationes* (wild beast games), and 10,000 gladiators in the *munera* (gladiatorial games), some of whom may have been Dacian prisoners of war. According to the historian Cassius Dio (AD163–235), the combined games occupied 123 days but were spread out over nearly two years to avoid sating the Roman public's demand for bloodshed and bankrupting the exchequer.

Trajan was the second of the five 'Good Emperors' who gave the Roman Empire nearly a century of general peace and prosperity. Trajan's successor Hadrian (AD117–138), who abandoned his predecessor's untenable conquests in Iraq, also gave lavish games, as did his successor Antoninus Pius (AD138–161).

The next ruler, Marcus Aurelius (AD161–180), the 'philosopher-emperor' – his *Meditations* remain a classic of Stoic philosophy – had absolutely no interest in the *munera*.

▼ *A mosaic from around AD250 from the Roman colony of Bad Kreuznach, Germany, showing gladiators fighting. The games were popular right across the empire. (Mary Evans)*

He used to deal with his letters and petitions while in the imperial box, hardly glancing at the arena. Yet, Marcus still felt obliged to put on regular shows at the amphitheatre. He did, however, try to make them more humane by encouraging gladiators to use padded swords in the actual fights – such swords were already used in training – to reduce the carnage,

A QUESTION OF SOURCES

For details of the building and workings of the Colosseum we have several conflicting texts. The three most important are *The Twelve Caesars* by the historian Suetonius, *Roman History* by Cassius Dio and the *Historia Augusta*.

Suetonius (AD69–140) worked as private secretary to the emperor Hadrian before being dismissed for misbehaving towards the empress Sabina. (Allegedly Suetonius had seduced Sabina, for Hadrian was not interested in women.) With his unrivalled access to the imperial archives, plus the reports of many eyewitnesses, Suetonius wrote his scandalous biographical history *The Twelve Caesars* covering the emperors up to Domitian. These are highly readable and very intelligent.

Next was Cassius Dio (AD155–235) who had the fortune – or misfortune – to live through the reign of Commodus that he so vividly described. Coming from the Greek East, he was a senator and minister in the imperial government in the AD220s. His *Roman History* described Rome's evolution from mythical times down to his own consulship in AD193, but only fragments of the text survive.

Lastly, both chronologically and in terms of reliability, is the *Historia Augusta*. The anonymous author who lived around AD400 mingled gossip and fantasy with fragments of solid history. It can be hard to tell one from the other.

THE COLOSSEUM'S IMITATORS AND PROGENY

Across the growing empire amphitheatres were erected even in the furthest provinces. Some 200 of these were clearly inspired by the mother of all amphitheatres in Rome, the Colosseum.

There were amphitheatres based on this model at Chester in Northwest England and at Caerleon in South Wales. Both were small oval arenas with plain, stone walls, and earth and timber embankments – there was no money for marble or gilt decorations on the military frontiers of the empire. Both were close to legionary camps as soldiers loved gladiatorial combats, although full-scale gladiatorial fights in these small arenas were rare because of the expense.

In contrast, wealthy cities such as Arles in southern France had much grander amphitheatres and could afford to host lavish *munera*. The building of Arles' arena started in AD90 and it still looms over the city today. Its stylistic debt to the Colosseum, using columns punctuated by arches, is obvious. It seats only 20,000 people, but its capacity is large relative to the size of Arles, which had less than a tenth of Rome's 1 million inhabitants. Similar amphitheatres were erected in other provinces, from Germany to Africa. One at El Djem in modern Tunisia, started around AD200 when Roman Africa was at its most prosperous, looks exactly like a scaled down Colosseum.

▶ *The amphitheatre at El Djem in Tunisia, built around AD200, resembles the Roman arena closely.*

▲ *The amphitheatre at Arles, begun in AD90, copied its Roman prototype on a smaller scale, seating only 20,000. Dramatic performances are still given in it.*

but this idea did not catch on. In truth, one of the major attractions of the *munera* for the Romans was the huge amount of blood shed at each event.

At the games emperor and people could confront and appraise each other face to face across the arena. If Rome was no longer in any way a democracy – although elections for officials such as consuls and praetors actually continued until AD19 – at least the people of Rome could voice their approval or disapproval of their emperor when they faced him inside the amphitheatre with an intimacy impossible elsewhere.

Aware of this, Augustus, the first emperor (reigned 27BC–AD14), always made a point of attending the games and watching the major events closely. This was partly to indicate that he was a man of the people who loved the sport, as a modern politician might do by supporting a football team. Also, as the emperor was by then very often the sole *editor*, the man who actually paid for the show, he wanted to gauge and enjoy the public's gratitude. Augustus's example was followed by most of the later emperors. Although the reclusive Tiberius (AD14–37) seldom attended shows – an absence that was noted and caused resentment – his half-mad heir Gaius Caligula not only attended the games but also liked to dress as a gladiator,

though normally only in private. Nero, the playboy prince, also sometimes played at being a gladiator, among the many other roles he affected.

Commodus (AD180–192), the successor, and officially the son of Marcus Aurelius – strong rumour had it that his real father had been a gladiator – took the games far more seriously. He actively participated in many *venationes*, killing thousands of animals. Commodus was finally assassinated for his megalomania – he wanted to rename Rome after himself – and increasingly murderous paranoia. His death led to a new round of civil wars until the final victory of Septimius Severus (AD193–211), first of the new Severan dynasty who ruled AD193–235. Septimius is noted in gladiatorial history for his ban in AD200 on women gladiators, although these shows had always been something of an oddity.

Through all changes of dynasty, as the empire grew richer and larger, the Colosseum's role as Rome's – and the empire's – premier place of public entertainment was unchallenged. The Circus Maximus might have been bigger – it could seat up to 300,000– and the Forum Romanum always retained its mystique as the ancient centre of Roman life, but the Colosseum had quickly become a famous landmark, indeed the very emblem of Rome.

GRADUAL DECLINE AND EVENTUAL DECAY

In the 3rd century AD Rome's fortunes started changing for the worse, and as if its fortunes were inextricably linked, a series of disasters also struck the amphitheatre. Some of these were natural disasters confined to the city, such as earthquakes or fire, but others were part of cultural and emotional changes in the empire as a whole.

LIGHTNING AND OTHER DISASTERS

On 23 August AD217 the Colosseum was struck by lightning and caught fire. This proved a major disaster, unlike a smaller lightning strike in AD146. Although the amphitheatre appeared to be solidly built of brick, stone and concrete, it had a lot of wood in both the top levels, which were mostly made of timber, and in the complex workings of the *hypogeum* below with its props, scenery and machinery, while the very shape of the *cavea* acted as a huge funnel to the flames.

The northwest part of the building suffered especially heavy damage, the outer part of the *cavea* between doors 40 and 47 needing rebuilding from the ground up. At the gladiators' entrance at the west end, fire damage went right into the basement while in the levels above ground a quarter of the circuit needed rebuilding. The *hypogeum* was also badly affected with many of its supporting walls collapsing. Cassius Dio, who was an eyewitness, described the event vividly if perhaps with a little exaggeration: the Romans were never very good at fire-fighting.

> The theatre was struck by thunderbolts on the very day of the Vulcanalia [mock volcanic explosions], and such a blaze followed that its whole upper circle and everything in the arena was burnt up. Then the rest of the building was ravaged by fire and reduced to ruin. Human attempts to control the blaze proved useless, although almost every aqueduct was emptied [of water], nor could violent downpours of rain check it.
>
> Cassius Dio

It took nearly 20 years to restore the Colosseum fully, although by AD222 work had advanced far enough for a ceremonial reopening. The emperor Alexander Severus (AD222–235) used taxes from the earnings of prostitutes who plied their trade beneath the arches of the ground level for the rebuilding. (These arcades, called *fornices*, reputedly are the origin of the English word fornication.) While the amphitheatre was shut, *munera* were held in the Circus Maximus.

POLITICAL UPHEAVAL

The assassination of Alexander Severus in AD235 marked the start of half a century of chaos for the empire. At least 30 emperors are officially recorded in this period, with the empire

▼ *The remains of the Circus Maximus, site of the chariot races and some* munera. *Rome's largest place of popular entertainment pre-dated the Colosseum by centuries. Behind it rise the ruins of the Palatine Palace.*

at times being split between warring rulers. Barbarians soon crossed the undefended frontiers to threaten the Eternal City – as it was increasingly being called, for it had stood unconquered for so long – for the first time in more than 600 years. Yet the celebration of Rome's millennium in AD248 was marked by games of great splendour, which went smoothly. They were held, of course, in the Colosseum.

A major earthquake that hit Rome in AD262 may have shaken the great building but it was evidently in good working order when the emperor Aurelian (AD270–275) hosted a series of games there in AD274. This was to celebrate victories that had just restored the eastern provinces and Gaul (France) to Roman control. Aurelian also ordered the hasty construction of walls around the city after three centuries when the city had stood proudly open. These still stand in parts and bear his name.

In AD284, Diocletian became emperor and set about remoulding the empire into a new system that we now call the Tetrarchy (four rulers system). He chose four new capitals, among them Milan and Trier, for himself and his three junior rulers. Much closer to the endangered frontiers, these cities effectively deprived Rome of its role as the political and administrative capital of the empire. It remained, however, the sacred Eternal City and grand ceremonial centre, its citizens still pampered with plentiful free entertainment and food. *Munera* in the Colosseum continued despite all the empire's external problems.

FROM ROME TO BYZANTIUM

In AD284 Diocletian became emperor. In his rule of 21 years he transformed the empire more radically than any emperor since Augustus. He set it on the way to becoming what we now call the Byzantine Empire, although contemporaries never used the term.

Eastern and Western empires

Diocletian first divided the empire administratively between two equal emperors, each called an Augustus. The emperor in the West was based in Milan or Trier in the Moselle Valley, and the emperor in the East had his administrative capital in the Balkans or western Asia Minor. Diocletian then added two junior emperors, called caesars. The aim was to have an imperial ruler always ready to lead the armies when invasion threatened. The 'Roman Empire', however, remained very much one empire. There could only be one empire, for there was only one Rome.

When each 'Augustus' retired – as Diocletian uniquely did – his caesar would automatically become the Augustus, appointing a new caesar beneath him. The system was meant to function like a machine, averting the civil wars that had plagued the Roman world for half a century. It did not work, for when Diocletian was no longer determining matters, the various emperors began fighting each other again.

One of Diocletian's reforms did survive, however: the increase in the visible majesty and ritual formality of the rulers' courts. Augustus, the very first emperor, had liked to pretend that he was merely the top magistrate, first among equals. He would walk to the Senate House to greet senators, for example, although he always kept real power firmly in his hands. Under Diocletian, courtiers now approached the imperial throne kneeling, while eunuchs – who had all once been slaves – often acted as ministers. The Persian monarchy is thought to have inspired Diocletian's approach. When Constantine became sole emperor in AD324, he increased this courtly ritual yet further, completing the ruler's transformation into a truly imperial role. Even more important, Constantine founded

► *This huge marble head of Constantine I once belonged to an immense statue that stood in the Basilica Nova in Rome. Constantine's conversion to Christianity led in the longer term to the end of the munera.*

a permanent new capital on the Bosphorus. This city, formerly the small Greek port of Byzantium, was no mere administrative base but a proper imperial capital that Constantine endowed with new buildings, including a senate house, baths, palaces and a hippodrome. It had no amphitheatre, however, for Constantine as the first Christian emperor disapproved of the *munera*. Constantine wanted this city to be called New Rome. In fact it was soon known as Constantinople (today it is Istanbul, having become a mainly Turkish city after the Ottoman conquest in 1453).

At first Constantinople and Rome were the twin capitals of the Roman Empire, which at times was divided, at times united. After AD395, when Theodosius I split the empire between his two sons, it was never again reunited, though this had not been Theodosius' intention. Rome increasingly became a majestic ruin while Constantinople boomed. In the AD530s this Eastern Roman Empire even effected a partial reconquest of the Western Empire. After AD600, when Greek finally replaced Latin as the Eastern Roman Empire's official language and Arab conquests stripped the Empire of its outer provinces, it became what we now call the Byzantine empire. As such it developed a distinctive non-classical Christian culture that influenced both the Islamic and western Christian worlds.

THE END OF THE GAMES

The real threat to the Colosseum's role came from Christianity, which had been growing in strength throughout the times of trouble. Most Christians knew Roman arenas not as spectators but as victims of the periodic persecutions that had seen them martyred in arenas around the empire for refusing to abjure their faith. Martyrs' joyful acceptance of their fates, some of them possibly in the Colosseum's arena, reached a climax in the Great Persecution of Diocletian and Galerius of AD306– 310. By steadfastly refusing to deny their faith, these martyrs finally convinced the emperors that persecution was futile. They also impressed many fellow citizens, who had earlier been very hostile.

STATE RELIGION

In AD312 Constantine, the new caesar of the West, won the Battle of the Milvian Bridge outside Rome. He did so 'under the sign of the Cross'. That is, his soldiers reputedly wore the Christian XP emblem (the first two initials of Christ in Greek), hastily adopted after Constantine had dreamt the night before battle that his soldiers would 'conquer under that sign'. Constantine's victory led him to accept Christianity as his chosen religion, so starting its slow conquest of the empire. In AD313 Constantine and his co-emperor Licinius issued the Edict of Milan that granted tolerance for all religions to every citizen. By AD337, when Constantine died, Christianity was well on its way to becoming the empire's main religion.

Early Christians, who were often ascetics, disliked almost all public entertainments, including the theatre, but they especially hated gladiatorial games. Tertullian (AD160–220), a

leading Christian writer, had called the Colosseum 'a temple consecrated to demons'. By 'demons' Tertullian meant the pagan gods – most early Christians believed they existed and were actively malevolent – and his accusation was indeed true. The *munera* were religious in origin and statues of Rome's gods looked down on the arena.

Soon bishops began urging the first Christian emperor to ban the *munera*. Constantine, however, had to tread carefully. Most of his subjects were not yet Christians and they loved the games. He banned crucifixion as a punishment for obvious religious reasons both inside and outside the arena, and forbade courts from sending criminals to gladiatorial schools. Instead, the condemned men were to be worked to death in mines – not perhaps an improvement from their viewpoint.

In AD330 Constantine founded a resplendent new capital for the now unified empire on the Bosphorus, renaming the old city of Byzantium Constantinople after himself. (Today it is Istanbul). The city was intended to be the new Rome, with a new senate, palaces, aqueducts, walls, baths, colonnades and a hippodrome (circus for chariot races) – but no amphitheatres. Gladiatorial combat was not to be a hallmark of the new Christian empire, although chariot races would enthral crowds in Constantinople for centuries.

Despite increasing government disfavour and growing pressure to convert, paganism and all its customs, including the *munera,* took a long time to die, especially in Rome itself. Not until AD391 did the emperor Theodosius I (AD379–395) ban public worship of the old gods. Even then the *munera* continued, although it was growing ever harder to find suitable animals or humans for the arena.

Symmachus, a wealthy Roman aristocrat and diehard pagan, in AD393 hosted games in honour of his son becoming a praetor, a senior post, so reviving an old custom. He spent a fortune procuring wild animals such as antelopes, gazelles, leopards, lions and bears, but most proved too sickly to fight well on the day. All the 29 Saxon captives, who were scheduled as the main gladiators, committed suicide in their cells the night before rather than fight each other, leaving the combat to a few free volunteers. This fiasco proved prophetic.

◄ *Telemachus paid with his life for trying to stop the games in* AD*405. Within 30 years the* munera *had ended. (Getty)*

▲ *The sack of Rome by the Visigoths in* AD*410 was relatively gentle, but the Vandals' attack in* AD*455 was ruthless and rapacious. By then the* munera *had ceased. (Mary Evans)*

In AD405 a monk called Telemachus leapt into the arena to try to separate the combatants mid fight. He was killed in the attempt but his martyrdom, as it was soon seen, further tarnished the image of the *munera* and the emperor Honorius

AN AWE-STRUCK EMPEROR

Constantius II (AD337–361), the most successful of Constantine I's fratricidal sons, visited Rome for the first and only time in AD357. Although familiar with the splendours of Constantinople, the emperor was overwhelmed by what he saw. He marvelled at the public baths 'almost the size of provinces'; the Pantheon 'large as a shapely city-district, vaulted over in soaring beauty'; the Forum of Trajan 'unique in the whole world, something even the gods would regard as a wonder'; and the Colosseum, 'the huge bulk of the amphitheatre reinforced with its framework of travertine stone, so high that one can hardly see its top'.

Constantius gave chariot races in the Circus Maximus but no *munera* in the Colosseum, instead issuing further restrictions on who could be forced to fight in them. The Romans were still impressed by his careful air of divine remoteness – he held himself as rigid as if he were a statue made of ivory – by his exotic-looking troops, with their dragon-shaped banners that hissed in the wind and his Persian-style cavalry completely covered in gleaming armour, men and horses alike. The armies on which Rome now depended for its survival hardly seemed Roman at all.

(AD395–423) issued an edict against further games. Like most of Honorius' actions this edict seems to have had little effect but economic, religious and political factors finally combined to end the gladiatorial games. The last of Rome's archetypal games was probably held in AD433.

THE COLOSSEUM AND THE FALL OF ROME

Theodosius I was the last powerful Roman emperor to rule both the East and West. His feeble son Honorius proved incapable of defending the Western Empire against either barbarian attacks or civil war. Most of Honorius's heirs were equally incompetent, and in their paranoia tended to undermine rather than assist the desperate efforts of their generals to save the Western Empire. (The eastern half of the empire based in Constantinople, which we now call Byzantine, had better luck in its rulers and survived intact after some difficult decades.)

In AD410 the Visigoths under their king Alaric sacked Rome after a short siege. The Visigoths stayed only three days and proved relatively gentle conquerors – they escorted nuns to the safety of churches, for example, and left most buildings intact. However, the shock to Roman self-esteem was tremendous. The Eternal City, centre of the world, had fallen for the first time in 800 years. Although urban life soon recovered pretty well, the Colosseum itself being partly restored in AD417–423, province after province now slipped out of Roman control.

In AD455 the Vandals, a Germanic tribe who had already conquered North Africa, landed in central Italy with a fleet. They spent two weeks rapaciously stripping Rome of much of its treasures – hence the English term 'vandalise' – before sailing off with their booty. This plunder included the gilded roofs of many temples, which left the buildings exposed to the elements. The Vandals may also have taken the Menorah that Titus had looted from the Holy of Holies in the Temple of Jerusalem in AD70.

COLOSSEUM OR COLISEUM?

When the new amphitheatre was inaugurated in AD80 by the emperor Titus, it was called the Amphitheatrum Flavium or Flavian amphitheatre, after the dynasty that had commissioned it. It has become generally known as the Colosseum – or alternatively Coliseum – in more recent ages. The first spelling echoes the nickname of the huge statue of Helios the Sun God that once stood nearby: Colossus, male rather than neuter, of course. The second (incorrect) spelling comes from the lyrical description of the city and its amphitheatre by the Venerable Bede. Bede (AD673–735) was a Northumbrian holy man and scholar who has become known as the Father of English history. Bede had mistaken the etymology, thinking the arena was once a temple and its name derived from the Latin word for worship, *colo/colere*. This variant of the name later became common in English-speaking circles – it is what Byron always called it. Coliseum is also the name of the huge opera house or music hall in London designed by Frank Matcham that opened in 1904. This Coliseum was the largest such public venue at the time and its interior decor self-consciously invoked its great Roman precursor, although it is not of course oval. But the Colosseum itself, when it was functioning fully, was simply called the Amphitheatre by Roman citizens, for there was no other amphitheatre in Rome.

DECAY AND DECLINE

The Colosseum itself seems to have been little damaged although the nearby statue of the Colossus was possibly carried off in the sack. (Alternatively, it might already have been toppled by earthquakes, the fate that had levelled its famous namesake in Rhodes in 226BC.) Certainly earthquakes in AD429 and AD443 damaged the topmost levels of the amphitheatre, causing parts of them to collapse in on to the *cavea* and arena. It seems likely that the rubble from this fall was never properly removed and the arena now began to silt up.

The Colosseum had begun its long decline. But, unlike the empire that had produced it, it was to survive nearly intact to become the great symbol of the Eternal City.

> Let Memphis [in Egypt] keep quiet about the
>   barbarous splendours of their pyramids,
> And let the Assyrians not boast of Babylon's mighty
>   buildings;
> Let us not praise the effeminate Ionians because of
>   their famed temple of Diana…
> Don't let the Carians glorify the Mausoleum rising up
>   into the empty air:
> All these works /should yield to Caesar's great
>   amphitheatre.
> Fame will prefer it to all of the other buildings listed
>   above.
>
> Martial, *Liber Spectaculorum*, CAD83

▼ *The Colosseum at night, now skilfully illuminated, is a majestic and and also haunting building. Although only a little of its facade remains intact, the strength of its design is still overpowering.*

2

DESIGN
AND
CONSTRUCTION

CLASSICAL THEATRES

The great bulk of the Colosseum has dominated the ancient centre of Rome for nearly 2,000 years. Its elliptical shape and classical details seem so perfect that it is now hard to imagine any other type of amphitheatre. But the Colosseum was in many ways a radically new building in its time. Not only was it larger than all earlier amphitheatres, but its builders also deployed some novel engineering techniques and architectural motifs. Even its shape, a not quite perfect oval, was innovatory.

THE FIRST AMPHITHEATRES

While the Colosseum became acknowledged as the supreme amphitheatre, its design was not without precedents. Several provincial Italian cities had erected permanent arenas well before the Flavian emperors. These must have influenced the architects of the great Roman arena.

Amphitheatres, which differ from theatres in their function, call for a different form. A hemicycle is perfect for plays but an elliptical or oval arena is better suited for staging *munera*

▼ *The Theatre of Pompey in Rome, shown here in imaginative reconstruction, was the city's largest and most resplendent theatre, seating 27,000 spectators. (Alamy)*

(gladiatorial contests) and *venationes* (animal shows) where the action shifts rapidly around the whole arena. The oval amphitheatre seems to have originated in Campania to the south of Rome, probably because gladiatorial games were pioneered by the Oscans, an Italic (non-Latin) people living there.

The Etruscans, who influenced early Roman culture in many ways, also held *munera*. Based in central Italy, the Etruscans had outlying settlements in Campania. Many early *munera* in Rome were held in the Forum Romanum within a roughly elliptical wooden arena specially erected for each performance. Evidence of a *hypogeum*, the substructure required for staging complex games, has been found beneath the Forum.

BUILDING AN ALL-ROUND THEATRE

No earlier amphitheatre had looked exactly like the Colosseum. But all later arenas erected in the empire's major cities were clearly inspired by this archetypal amphitheatre in both their decoration and construction, as have been many more recent buildings, from sports stadia to opera houses.

The word *amphitheatre*, which means 'double' or 'all-round' theatre, reveals something about the building's origins. The Greeks had created the world's first true theatres, huge semi-circular open auditoria, by excavating mountain or hill slopes. This provided a relatively easy and cheap way of providing tiers of seats for large audiences in the *cavea* (auditorium), letting every citizen attend the dramatic performances so central to Greek life.

The Romans copied Greek theatres but adapted them for their high-density urban life. The Romans preferred to build theatres inside their cities and from the ground up, raising tiers of brick, stone and concrete vaults to create the *cavea,* rather than excavating a slope outside the city walls. This method did away with the need to find a suitable hillside into which the hemicycle of a Greek-style theatre could fit. So, Roman theatres and amphitheatres could be built wherever there was a demand for them.

Theatrum Marcelli

Much of the Theatre of Marcellus, situated nearby the Theatre of Pompey, remains intact – part of it is in fact now luxury flats. Dedicated in 11BC by Emperor Augustus to the memory of his son-in-law Marcellus who had died young, it seated around 11,000 people. Its *cavea* was supported on vaulted substructures built partly of cut stone and partly of *opus reticulatum*, a type of concrete covered in small square-faced stones. These concrete barrel vaults produced a radiating network of ascending ramps and *ambulacria*, ring-like corridors that allowed spectators to reach and leave their tiered seats easily.

▲ *Taormina's theatre is Greek in its original plan but its superstructure is wholly Roman. It offers stunning views of Mount Etna in Sicily.*

Externally the theatre's facade once had three rows of arches, each arch being framed by columns: Doric columns on the ground floor, Ionic on the first floor and probably Corinthian on the top. This uppermost row has now completely vanished. Both structurally and decoratively therefore, the Theatre of Marcellus anticipated major aspects of the Colosseum on a smaller scale, although work on the amphitheatre did not start until more than 80 years later.

▼ *The Theatre of Marcellus was dedicated by Emperor Augustus. Its facade anticipates that of the Colosseum.*

EARLY AMPHITHEATRES

The Colosseum in Rome has become so embedded in the popular imagination as the ultimate, supreme and archetypal amphitheatre that it is easy to forget that it was not built as the first or paradigmatic amphitheatre. By the time Titus inaugurated the Amphitheatrum Flavium many other cities around Italy had long had permanent amphitheatres; smaller and less elaborate than the great Roman building, perhaps, but they may well have influenced its design and construction.

AMPHITHEATRE OF POMPEII

Pompeii in southern Italy has the earliest all-masonry amphitheatre to survive in good condition. This is due to the eruption of Vesuvius in AD79, the lava from which preserved the city like a time capsule.

Originally an Oscan town, Pompeii was resettled as a military colony for retired legionaries in 80BC. Soldiers much enjoyed gladiatorial games, which probably explains the size of the arena. It could seat about 20,000, more than the population of the whole town at its peak, although by the time of its destruction Pompeii had ceased to be a barracks and had become in effect a holiday resort. As no holiday for Romans was complete without games, its arena, erected in c70BC and later embellished and reinforced against earthquakes, proved very popular with people in the region.

What is most striking about Pompeii's amphitheatre is its external plainness. (That this was the case with the original building is revealed by a mural that was discovered in a house in Pompeii showing it during the riots of AD59). It has almost no decorative features, apart from the blind arches of the

▼ *Theatres in the Greek world were the precursors of Roman amphitheatres. The theatre at Epidaurus in the Peloponnese has superb acoustics and plays are still put on there.*

▲ The amphitheatre at Pompeii, a military colony founded by the Republican general Sulla in c80BC which later became a pleasure resort. Almost intact thanks to the eruption of Mt Vesuvius in AD79, which covered the whole town in lava, Pompeii is the first all-masonry amphitheatre to survive. This could seat about 20,000 spectators, which was probably more than the population of the town at its peak just before its destruction. People from nearby towns must have supplied many of the spectators. Much of the cavea is now grassed over but it once held tiers of seats.

circuit wall, probably because it was built fast and by military engineers. The castra, the Romans' famous military forts, were also built quickly and were equally unadorned.

The design of the Pompeii amphitheatre was simple too. Earth was dug out to create the arena and the middle and lower tiers of the cavea, and was then piled up outside to support the seating for the summa cavea, the topmost tier of seats. The concrete façade of the building created a retaining wall for the spoils from this excavation. A canvas velarium (awning) to protect spectators is visible in the mural.

Two vaulted corridors under the seating, one on the main axis and the other at right angles to fit in with the adjacent city walls, allowed easy entry and exit for the performers. The spectators came and went by two double staircases and two single staircases on the perimeter wall. This may have created

▶ Top right: The interior of the arena at Pompeii. As it was one of the very earliest permanent amphitheatres, with a solid floor, it lacked the more elaborate features of later Roman arenas, such as subterranean tunnels and machinery.
Middle right: Spectators entered and left the arena by two double staircases and two single staircases on the perimeter wall. This restricted access may have caused problems with crowd control that were solved at the Colosseum.
Bottom right: Part of the vaulted corridor that ran around the arena beneath the tiered seats.

THE CLASSICAL ORDERS

Columns were essential elements of ancient architecture as they were to be again after the Renaissance from around 1400 onwards. Columns were used chiefly for structural purposes in classical Greek architecture but mainly as decoration in Roman buildings of the imperial era (after 31BC).

There are three principal types or 'orders' of column in both Greek and Roman architecture: the Doric, Ionic and Corinthian, all theoretically based on the proportions of the human body. They were categorised by Vitruvius, Augustus's great architect, in his influential book *On Architecture* written in *c*30BC.

The Doric was the simplest and shortest, with a plain capital (head).

The Ionic, which was longer and more elegant, had *volutes* (spiral scrolls) at the capitals' corners.

The Corinthian was around the same length as the Ionic but still more ornate, with two rows of acanthus leaves and other complex decorations around the capital.

Two further orders, the Tuscan, a rather stocky Italian variant of Doric, and the rather decadently ornate Composite appeared under the Romans.

In the Colosseum all the three first canonical orders of columns used are 'engaged', meaning half-sunk into the walls. This reveals that their role was purely decorative (*ie* they did not support the structure in any way). In porticoes and colonnades, however, the Romans continued to use columns for structural as well as decorative purposes.

▼ *The three 'orders' of classical columns in their Greek forms (top) and Roman versions (bottom).*

Doric	Ionic	Corinthian

◄ *Mount Vesuvius as seen from the ruins of Pompeii. The volcano had been dormant for thousands of years when Pompeii, originally an Etruscan and then an Oscan city, rose and flourished. The fertile volcanic soil and pleasant climate made that part of southern Italy especially attractive later to Roman settlers, who seem to have been totally unaware of the potential dangers Vesuvius posed until the fateful day of the eruption in August AD79. Excavations, which began in the 18th century, have since revealed an astonishingly well-preserved town.*

problems of crowd control at the beginning and end of the games, a problem solved in the more sophisticated Colosseum. Pompeii's arena with its solid core also lacked subterranean passages for machinery or trapdoors to permit the staging of elaborate *munera*. This was less of a problem for a small town that could seldom have afforded anything too elaborate.

The immense popularity of the amphitheatre at Pompeii was initially at least in part due to the presence of the numerous retired legionaries in Sulla's newly founded military colony. The parallels between combat in military life and those in the arena were obvious. Many ex-soldiers must have relished watching the fights from the comfortable safety of benches in the *cavea* – especially those between swordsmen – even more than most Roman civilians did.

Although in emergencies gladiators at times were recruited directly into the army – most notably during the crisis of AD168, when the army was badly hit by an outbreak of plague and lacked the troops to repel German invaders of Italy – their skills did not always prove fully transferable. Legionaries fought as members of highly disciplined units and were bound by an iron

▼ *The amphitheatre at Verona in northern Italy was built around AD50. Larger than that at Pompeii, it was also more elaborate, both in its decorative rows of pillars on its facade and in its* hypogeum *underneath the arena. It possibly inspired the unknown architects of the Colosseum a generation later.*

discipline, while gladiators almost always fought as individuals. Gladiators' skills as fighters, although indisputable, were essentially those of theatrical performers designed to impress the watching crowds. Legionaries fought as highly efficient cogs in Rome's overwhelmingly impressive army, making for a far less colourful form of combat. The remarkable early successes of Spartacus against several Roman armies in 73–71BC, however, shows that gladiators could, if properly led and motivated, combine to fight as an army.

VERONA ARENA

Verona in northern Italy was a very different city, much larger, richer and far more important than Pompeii. Among its other claims to fame, it had been the birthplace of the great lyric poet Catullus (84–54BC). Its amphitheatre, which was probably erected 120 years later than Pompeii's some time around AD50 – the exact date is still debated, some people inclining to a date 30 or so years later – shows much greater complexity. Rising to three stories – all earlier amphitheatres had had only two – it anticipates the Flavian's grand amphitheatre in several other ways.

With exterior measurements originally of 152 by 123m (500 by 405ft), Verona's was the third-largest arena in the empire, after Capua's and Rome's. It would probably have seated around 25,00 spectators. Built wholly of masonry, its free-standing structure has some notable features in common with the Colosseum. Dressed stone makes up the main network of vaulted corridors, with *opus caementicium* (Roman concrete) playing a smaller and less visible part. Pinkish stone from nearby Valpolicella was carved for the square pilasters on the lower two tiers to create an external facade of 72 arches, each spanning 2m/6ft 6in. These arches gave access to an interior corridor 4.4m/13ft 6in wide running around the arena. This in turn led to a radiating web of tunnels and galleries that allowed the entry and exit of the spectators on four levels via *vomitoria*. There are also traces of a *hypogeum*, which would

▼ *The interior of the arena of Verona's amphitheatre today, with seating that is far better preserved than that in the Colosseum, allowing it to host operatic spectacles.*

have permitted subterranean machinery, beneath the central arena. (The word arena itself comes from *harena*, the Latin for 'sand'. The floors of amphitheatres were typically covered in sand during performances.)

Verona's amphitheatre as built had three tiers of arched windows, each flanked by columns or pilasters. Originally the façade reached a height of around 30m/100ft, but today only two tiers survive except in one small portion where four arches remain of the top tier. The uppermost tier's arched openings did not form the arches of an encircling gallery but were actual decorative windows that rose high above the seats. The same arrangement, decorative rather than functional, applies to the amphitheatre at Pola.

Unlike its Roman counterpart, which proudly displays all the main three classical orders (Doric, Ionic, Corinthian), the two lower tiers' columns at Verona are in the simpler, less common Tuscan style. This might have been because the emperor Claudius, in whose reign (AD41–54) the amphitheatre was probably built, personally favoured the Tuscan order. It was thought a distinctly Roman as opposed to Greek style

▲ *The limestone facade of the amphitheatre in Pula, Croatia, is similar in design to the roughly contemporary arena at Verona but is better preserved externally.*

▼ *The interior of the amphitheatre in Pula, showing it arranged for a live performance.*

and Claudius was a keen Roman traditionalist – one reason he was such a fan of the *munera* themselves.

Inside Verona's amphitheatre seats are arranged in four elliptic rings, producing a total of 44 rows of benches. The drainage system, which is still partly functioning, was extensive and has helped preserve the amphitheatre remarkably well. The arena also had the great good fortune of having an endowment fund established in the 13th century for its maintenance. By that time its original gory pagan functions had long been forgotten and the amphitheatre was seen as having almost mystical qualities, due to it being built by saints according to medieval legends. Today the arena hosts a

grand opera season in the summer. Its acoustics have turned out to be surprisingly good, although it was certainly not designed for any sort of operatic performances.

PULA AMPHITHEATRE

The amphitheatre at Pula (Pola) – a coastal city now in Croatia but in Roman times an integral part of Italy – was first built as a timber structure in the early 1st century AD. It was rebuilt in stone around AD60 and then extended under Vespasian or Titus in AD77–80. A coin from Vespasian's reign found in the structure helps date its final phase. Reputedly a Christian martyr called Germanus was killed in the arena early in the 4th

century. During the Middle Ages it suffered the fate common to many large Roman public buildings of being used as a quarry for cut stone. More unusually, it was also used as a jousting ground. But restoration began under the Napoleonic occupation in the early 19th century, a process that continued when Pula passed under Austrian rule after 1815.

Today Pula has one of the best-preserved amphitheatres in the Roman world. Its grand facade, made of the pale local limestone, still rises to three stories on the seaward

▼ *The interior of the grandest amphitheatre of them all as it appears today, most of it now exposed to the elements.*

▲ *Statue of the Emperor Titus who oversaw the inauguration ceremonies of the Colosseum with games of unprecedented splendour and extravagance.*

▼ *A 19th-century Italian* quadriga *(four-horse chariot), modelled on the statues known to have topped the main entry arches to the Colosseum, long since vanished.*

▲ *The upper tier of the remaining outer wall of the Colosseum showing some of the 240 brackets or corbels, which originally held the tall wooden posts to support the awning that shaded the* cavea. *The Corinthian pilasters flank alternately square windows and now-blank wall spaces where bronze shields once hung, glittering in the sunlight.*

side although on the landward side only two stories survive. The first two tiers have 72 arches flanked by columns while the topmost floor has 64 simple square windows. As in the amphitheatre at Verona, the pilasters between the arches are relatively shallow, which makes the arches stand out as the main decorative feature. This contrasts with the Colosseum,

where flamboyant columns dominate the façade. The walls at Pula rise to 32.5m/107ft. The amphitheatre when functioning could seat up to 23,000 spectators in the *cavea*, which had 40 rows of seating. The arena itself measures about 70 by 42m/223 by 137ft, making it the sixth-largest amphitheatre in the Roman world.

The arena originally had 15 gates for gladiators and other combatants. A skeletal *hypogeum* has also been uncovered, suggesting that games of real complexity could be have been staged. A distinctive feature of Pula's amphitheatre is its four ceremonial entrance towers each containing a cistern in them, from which spectators were perhaps showered with scented water. This feature was not quite unique to Pula but has vanished from almost all other amphitheatres.

If none of these three earlier arenas in Italy could really match the splendour and grandeur of the Colosseum, the fine architectural features of the two northern ones show that the Flavian amphitheatre had important and significant precursors, which Vespasian would have wanted to match.

Egypt forbear thy Pyramids to praise,
A barbarous work up to a Wonder raise;
Let Babylon cease the incessant Toil to prize,
Which made her walls to such immensities rise...
All works to Caesar's Theatre give place,
This Wonder Fame above the rest does grace.

Martial, *Liber de Spectaculis*, trans.
Henry Killigrew *c*1670

◄ *A corridor in the* hypogeum, *the two-storied underworld that ran beneath the entire arena. From its depths, through trapdoors, emerged wild animals, scenery and other special effects. (Alamy)*

► *The Domus Aurea, Nero's lavish Golden Palace, is notable for its pioneering use of vaults and for its frescoes, fragments of which survive in this section of the underground ruin.*

ROMAN CONCRETE

Opus caementicum, Roman concrete, made the construction of the Colosseum and other huge vaulted buildings such as basilicas and baths possible. It also made them very durable. Roman concrete differs from modern concrete in that it creates what is really artificial stone, which is much quicker and easier to work with than real stone. *Opus caementicum* was not poured but laid by hand in rough horizontal courses between timber frames.

Inspired by examples from towns in Campania, the Romans were by 200BC using mortar made of lime and *pozzolana*, a black volcanic sand, to construct walls. They continued to develop and refine this over the centuries in a typically pragmatic process of trial and error. By Nero's reign architects and builders had at their disposal a uniquely adaptable, cheap and robust building material.

As *opus caementicum* was never reinforced with steel, as modern concrete is, it is unusually flexible. This has helped ancient domes and vaults to survive Italy's recurrent earthquakes better than many more recent buildings. The walls' cores were filled with small stones, producing a solid cohesive mass when mortar was laid on top. Rome had plenty of limestone in nearby quarries that could be burnt to produce the lime needed for the mortar. Vitruvius, the great architectural theorist, writing in *c*30BC recommended using three parts of volcanic sand to one part of mortar when erecting walls of *opus caementicum*.

Special types of *opus caementicum* were also developed that could set under water, which proved invaluable when building harbours. This sort of concrete was made of quicklime (calcium oxide) and volcanic ash. When seawater gets into its cracks, it causes a chemical reaction that strengthens the concrete, unlike modern concrete. Minerals called Al-tobermorite, a rare, hydrothermal, calcium-silicate-hydrate mineral, and phillipsite form as the matter leaks mineral-rich fluid. This then solidifies, reinforcing the concrete and making the structure even stronger. As the writer Pliny the Elder remarked: 'As soon as it comes into contact with the sea and is submerged, it becomes a single stone mass (*fierem unum lapidem*), impregnable to waves and growing stronger every day.' Exactly how the Romans produced such concrete is still unclear but it is being investigated. It could prove useful in dealing with floods.

▼ *Ruins of Caesarea, the capital Herod built in Judaea, using* opus caementicum *that could set under water.*

BUILDING THE COLOSSEUM

Exactly when construction on the Colosseum began is uncertain. It had probably started before AD75, perhaps as early as AD72 or as soon as Vespasian felt securely in power. Vespasian's motto was *Roma Resurgens* ('Rome revives') and the giant amphitheatre was the most obvious sign of its resurgence. Vespasian probably saw only the lower two tiers finished before his death in AD79. The main parts of the Colosseum were nearly complete by AD80. That year Titus gave the grand inaugural games in his dynasty's new amphitheatre so it was clearly functioning as an arena by then. Martial, however, mentions scaffolding was still up at the time, so it was not completed.

Domitian's long reign (AD81–96) saw the topmost tier, which was made mostly of wood, added and the *velarium* (awning) with its long poles erected on top of that. This extra superstructure would have made the amphitheatre appear even higher to onlookers. Far beneath, hidden from the spectators, the elaborate *hypogeum,* the subterranean labyrinth of tunnels for the animals, scenery and the machinery to lift them up, was built in Domitian's reign too, a reign that was even more architecturally daring than those of his father and brother. The *quadriga*, the statues of four-horsed chariots that stood above each entrance arch, probably dated from this period too. So too did the luxuriously painted stucco decorations that covered every part of the building. These, like other decorative features, have not survived. No expense was spared on the Flavian dynasty's hallmark.

LAYING THE FOUNDATIONS

The first requirement was to ensure that after rainstorms the site did not revert to what it had been earlier: a lake in a river valley. The elliptical shape of the building acted as a giant funnel that collected and channelled rainwater, aggravating the problem. During a heavy storm 175 litres/39gal per second could accumulate inside the *cavea*.

DRAINAGE

Fortunately, the principles of land drainage were well understood by Roman engineers. The Romans installed a highly effective drainage system around and beneath the centre of the amphitheatre. Recent excavations have uncovered a complex network of drains. The ring drain, which encircled the

▼ *The complex drainage system of the Colosseum was a vital part of construction because the huge structure was built mainly on the site of a former lake. A ring drain ran around the perimeter 8m/26ft underground, feeding four large water conduits that took the water that accumulated in the valley's base away to the distant Tiber river.*

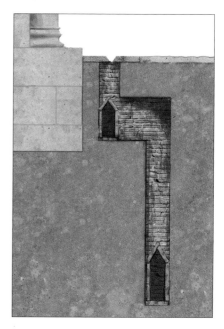

▼ *A cross-section of the subterranean external drainage system running around the Colosseum's circumference.*

▶ *The drainage system that kept the Colosseum from flooding was built at the same time as the foundations, by casting cement over wooden boxing over 50m/165 feet long.*

arena, ran 8m/26ft beneath the base of the valley to take water off into the Tiber via four large water conduits. Other conduits ran just beneath the travertine paving of the piazza outside, helping drain the main auditorium as well as the piazza. In total there were nearly 3,000m/3,330yd of channels and conduits in the amphitheatre.

The lead piping used – some of which would have fed water into the amphitheatre for the 20 fountains and the various toilets inside the structure – has all vanished, stolen during the long centuries of depredation after the fall of the empire. Siphons, a technique the Romans also used in their aqueducts and public baths, pumped water up to the higher levels.

After the site was cleared of the remains of Nero's palace – the massive foundations were mostly left in situ, as often happened with existing buildings – a vast trench was dug. This ran for 6m/19ft 6in under the bottom of the existing lake, penetrating 4m/13ft into the clay beneath. The trench created a doughnut-shaped ring that measured about 200m/666ft across the long axis and 156m/510ft across the shorter axis. Two concentric containing walls of brick-faced concrete, each 3m/9ft 9in thick and 6.5m/21ft 6in high, were built along this trench.

The space between these walls was then filled with concrete to just above the earlier lake level. Four gaps, each 5m/16ft 6in wide, were left in this perimeter for the four main entrances on each of the four axes and four tunnels with travertine walls and concrete vaults were built in the resulting gaps, with drainage conduits sloping outwards at an incline of 1:40. (The remains of the wooden shuttering used for the concrete pouring were found during excavations in the 1970s.) With the ground now level, a 40cm/16in layer of concrete was poured over what had been the lakebed.

The amphitheatre's concrete foundations were then laid. This layer was about 12m/40ft deep beneath the seating area and extended some 6m/19ft 6in outside the perimeter. The great depth was needed to support the huge weight of the tiered seats; under the arena the foundations were only about 6m/19ft 6in deep. On this platform a framework of piers of hard travertine stone from quarries at Tivoli was built in a series of concentric arches. These massive stone arches constituted the vital load-bearing skeleton of the whole building up to the arches of the second tier. Between the travertine piers radial walls of tufa, a softer stone, were inserted up to the second tier. Above this, level brick-

▶ *The cross-section of the north-eastern side of the Colosseum shows its foundations and superstructure. Inset: The travertine substructures beneath the facade.*

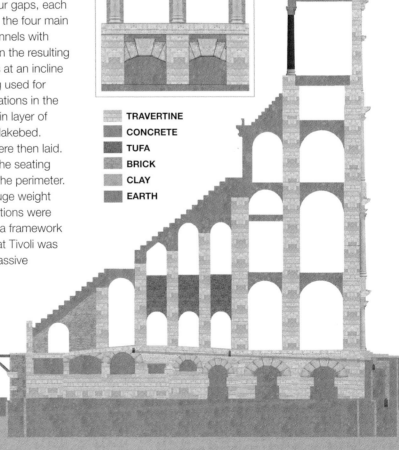

- TRAVERTINE
- CONCRETE
- TUFA
- BRICK
- CLAY
- EARTH

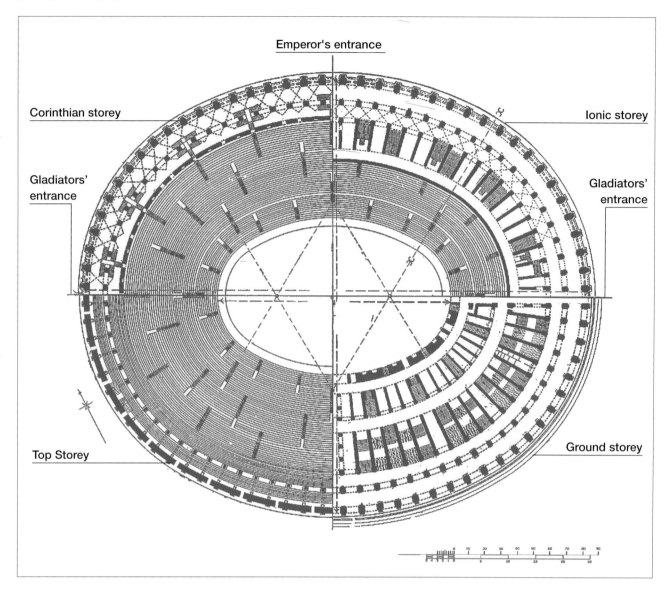

Emperor's entrance

Corinthian storey

Ionic storey

Gladiators' entrance

Gladiators' entrance

Top Storey

Ground storey

▲ *A bird's-eye-view diagram of the Colosseum's floors. The ground or entrance level's great circle of arches is flanked by Doric columns, most of which still exist intact. The next floor has Ionic columns, the next, Corinthian. The top level had square openings flanked by Corinthian pilasters.*

faced concrete, which was both lighter and easier to work, was used, except at the very top, which was built almost entirely of wood.

SOURCING AND TRANSPORTING MATERIALS

Building the Colosseum was an immense task. It entailed draining the lake of the Domus Aurea, removing some 220,000 tons of soil from the site and disposing of the spoils outside the city, usually by barge down the Tiber, although probably some earth was used to raise the ground level around the building. It then meant bringing in about 100,000c m/3,531,467c ft of hard travertine stone, the prime building material, plus lesser amounts of tufa and similar soft stone from the main quarries at Tivoli about 30km/20 miles from the city and from smaller

mines further away. Along with the stone, over 1 million bricks were transported by cart from the huge brickyards, most of them well up the Tiber. The river, unfortunately, is seldom navigable in its higher reaches. Finally the marble – from Carrara or from North Africa and Greece – the bronze, and wood, plus sand and stone for the *opus caementicum* (concrete), had to be brought into the heart of the city.

This massive construction work in the heart of the city created a constant stream of traffic through Rome's narrow streets. (It has never been a city of broad avenues, unlike ancient Alexandria or modern Paris and New York.) For nearly a decade lines of heavily laden ox-drawn carts, the Roman equivalent of trucks, trundled day and night towards the building site. As each cart could carry only half a ton at maximum and moved slowly at around 3kph/2mph, about half a million cartloads were needed. They must have disturbed and disrupted half of Rome on a 24-hour basis. No wonder that Vespasian had to suspend the laws passed by Julius Caesar that banned the use of wheeled vehicles inside the city during the day to ease congestion.

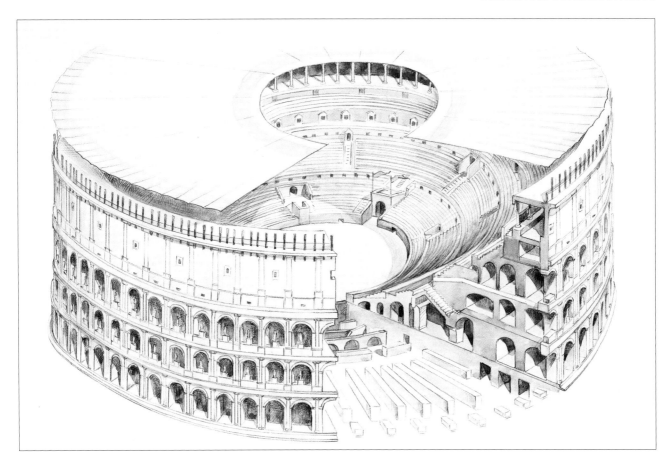

TIERED SEATING

The seating was terraced outwards and upwards on the ascending vaults of a grid of radiating stairways or ramps and lateral passages, all designed to give each class of spectator meticulously segregated access to their allotted wedge-shaped block (*cuneus*) of seats. Every seating block was further divided by horizontal gangways.

▲ *The Colosseum cut away to reveal the corridors, substructure and* hypogeum *after the alterations made under Domitian around* AD*90. It changed little in subsequent centuries. (Getty)*

As well as allowing for the easy lateral circulation of spectators, the outer annular passageways helped to support the outward thrust of the tiers of seating. Such almost casual

LABOURERS: SLAVE AND FREE

The traditional picture of the Colosseum being built by armies of slaves, mostly Jewish captives labouring under the overseers' lash, is misleading. During the Principate (31BC–AD285) the imperial system of building relied mainly on private enterprise. Builders, whether free or servile, skilled or unskilled, worked side by side for private contractors, usually small family-owned teams. Draughtsmen, surveyors, bricklayers, masons, carpenters, painters and sculptors made up much of this workforce. Many labourers were undoubtedly slaves but skilled craftsmen were usually free Roman citizens. Often they were enrolled in *collegia,* Rome's trade unions or guilds that ensured minimum levels of pay and working conditions. It has been estimated that building the Colosseum required at least 10,000 workers. At the height of construction this may have risen towards 20,000. This figure excludes the many men producing the raw materials: brick, stone, marble, concrete, iron, copper, bronze.

For nearly three centuries the building trade was the biggest source of work in the imperial capital, a city of chronic under-employment. (Ordinary Roman citizens depended heavily on the *annona,* the free grain ration handed out to all full male citizens – but not to slaves or foreigners – by the emperors. Lavish free entertainments and equally lavish free public baths were also essential for keeping Rome's volatile citizens content.) When an inventor suggested to Vespasian a new labour-saving device, the Emperor dismissed the man with a payment, saying he did not want to deprive the Roman people of work. Only in the mines, always considered hellish places, did slave workers almost totally displace the free. Here war captives, some of them doubtless Jewish, worked alongside other slaves. *Damnati* (condemned men) often preferred to take their chances in the arena rather than face the slow death that came from working underground.

ingenuity was typical of Roman architectural and engineering brilliance, then at its prime. The *cavea* at the Colosseum is actually almost vertiginously steep, rising at an angle of nearly 45 degrees – the amphitheatre was the ancient city's tallest building – but this is hardly apparent when inside, so well engineered are the tiers.

All the seats, except in the topmost two levels, were of carved marble carried on the substructures of vaulted masonry. Above this, in the *maenianum summum ligneum*, they were made of wood. This was intended to lessen the weight at the point where the outward thrust of the building was countered only by the thickness of the outer wall. Beneath this level the doubled ambulatory corridors and vaulted *vomitoria* created a massive system of buttressing that was more than enough to meet the stresses put upon it.

What is most surprising about surviving seats in Greek and Roman theatres and in amphitheatres is how comfortable they still are for spectators. This cannot of course be gauged in the Colosseum, where almost nothing of the original seating has survived (a small area has been reconstructed). But it can be experienced at Greek theatres such as Epidaurus and equally well in Roman amphitheatres such as Verona or Orange and Arles in southern France. Further, the acoustics are astonishingly good at all these sites. This suggests that ancient engineers and architects, although they never left manuals or notes for posterity, were as skilled and knowledgeable as modern builders at erecting huge buildings for mass audiences.

THE EXTERIOR WALLS AND DECORATION

The amphitheatre's exterior was even more lavishly decorated than the interior. When complete and intact, its four tiers of columns – engaged Doric, Ionic and Corinthian columns on the first three, flanking arches with statues of gods or heroes in each, with square Ionic pilasters on the topmost floor flanked by giant bronze shields – must have presented an astonishing vision. Like many of Rome's greatest buildings, the Colosseum demonstrated a fusion of Roman engineering know-how and innovation with Greek aesthetic brilliance.

The outer structure of the Colosseum was impressive enough a sight, but the complex and ingenious velarium above (huge sail-like awnings to shade the audience), and the other world beneath the sands of the arena, were just as impressive.

THE HYPOGEUM

Hidden from spectators but vital to staging the games in their violent glory: the *hypogeum* (underground chamber) was not an original feature of the Colosseum because of the need to flood the arena for *naumachia* (mock naval battles) in its first years. Many things about this complex underworld remain unclear, partly because clumsy 19th-century excavations damaged it but also because the *hypogeum* was repaired or rebuilt at least 12 times over its 300 years of use.

The following facts are certain: the *hypogeum* measured 75m/247ft long by 44m/145ft wide and extended on two

floors to 6m/19ft deep beneath the arena floor. The floor itself, mainly built of wood, beneath the constantly-refreshed sand, rested on a series of cantilevers which were set into the surrounding brickwork between the vaulted chambers. Travertine stone blocks, several of which have been discovered still in situ, were set into the basement floor at intervals of about 6 or 7m/19ft or 22ft. These huge pieces of masonry accommodated the wooden mounds about 6m/19ft high that supported the whole arena. Their immense spans of 6 or 7m/19ft or 22ft were fixed in the middle by trusses resting on two consoles.

In Domitian's reign (AD81–96), six straight walls of soft tufa stone 90cm/3ft wide were built parallel to the arena's

CARRARA MARBLE

The emperor Augustus liked to boast that he had found Rome a city of brick and left it a city of marble. His claim was nearly true, at least for great public buildings. Private dwellings, however, especially *insulae*, the tall, often rickety tenement blocks where most citizens lived, were built of plain brick and concrete, although the better blocks would have had some stucco decoration.

The marble used to adorn temples, basilicas, theatres and arches after 31BC was mostly Carrara marble. Usually a brilliant white, this came from the abundant quarries of Carrara, a town just north of Lucca in Tuscany. Quarrying there had begun in 48BC under Julius Caesar, who had wildly ambitious if unrealised plans for rebuilding Rome. It has continued ever since. While more expensive coloured marbles were also imported from North Africa and Greece, most public buildings in imperial Rome, including the Colosseum, were built of brick, concrete and stone and faced in marble, usually in Carrara marble or, for less important surfaces, stucco. The marble might itself be painted or the facing might be further adorned with gilt, bronze or silver statues. For the Romans, decoration was never a crime.

▼ *The Carrara marble quarries from which much of the marble for the Colosseum was dug. It is still in use today.*

▲ The Colosseum also contained a huge amount of brickwork, some of which has been exposed here. Tiles and bricks were made with clay mixed with water, sand, straw and finely ground pozzolana. They were dried in the sun before being fired, and were often used as filling within walls, as well as to tile roofs.

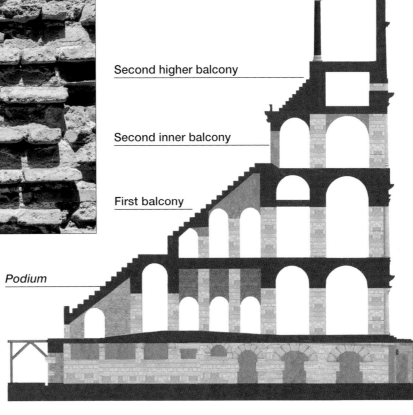

Second higher wooden balcony

Second higher balcony

Second inner balcony

First balcony

Podium

▼ Fresco from Herculaneum, well preserved thanks to Vesuvius's eruption, which suggests what decoration inside the Colosseum's entrance arches might have looked like.

▲ Diagrammatic cross-section of the Colosseum showing the different tiers of seats with their annular corridors running in rings. The arched substructure supported both the tiers of seating and the facade.

▼ Reconstruction of a vomitorium, an entrance to the cavea that 'vomited' forth crowds of spectators.

▼ *The Colosseum cut away to reveal the corridors, substructure and* hypogeum *after the alterations made under the emperor Domitian around* AD*90. It changed little in subsequent centuries.*

The *quadriga*, the four-horse statue above the ceremonial entrance (the *Porta Triumphalis)*

The *summa maenianum*, the only level in which women, other than vestal virgins, were allowed

The wooden posts that supported the *velarium* or awning

Vomitoria, the entrances and exits for the audience

The *podium*, the best seating on the lowest level, closest to the arena

The *pulvinar*, or imperial box

The *hypogeum*

Ambulacrum, or walkways, on each level

main axis along with three elliptical walls parallel to the perimeter walls. These walls, which have been much altered and repaired since Domitian's time, created corridors where the stage machinery was located. Probably prior to this construction the perimeter walls themselves had once contained small lifts to bring animals and scenery up into the arena. There may also have been four lifts at the ends of either side of the two long tunnels

There are numerous traces of the many alterations that the Colosseum's builders seem to have made to the great amphitheatre in its very early days. Traces of demolished walls on the floor of the basement suggest that the architects in the first years of operation may have suddenly recognised that more space was needed for lifts to permit the raising of large scenery and props, and possibly even for housing the boats that were for a brief period used in the *naumachia* or mock sea fights. Such radical changes to work in progress were common Roman building practice.

THE LIFT SYSTEM

Thirty-two lifts were installed in the narrow gaps 2m/6ft 6in wide between the tufa walls, and set in rectangular blocks of hard travertine, some of which still survive. These blocks have round holes in their middle and reveal traces of the bronze sockets of capstans that once fitted into the holes. Opposite each of the blocks there are shallow recesses in the walls that allowed the capstans to be turned.

Dr Heinz-Jürgens Beste of the German Archaeological Institute in Rome conducted extensive surveys of the *hypogeum* in the late 1990s and 2000s, the work hugely expanding our knowledge of its workings. According to Dr Beste, the *hypogeum* at the height of its operation had 60 capstans, each two floors high and turned by four men per

▶ *A reconstructed lift in the Colosseum's renovated* hypogeum *gives an idea of how they might have worked.*

▼ *A corridor in the* hypogeum *lined with blocks of travertine and a huge lintel with a giant keystone at its centre. (Getty)*

▲ *Interior of the* hypogeum *showing a layer of travertine, the limestone from Tivoli in which much of the load-bearing part of the Colosseum is constructed. (Alamy)*

level. Forty of these capstans lifted animal cages up to the arena, while the remaining 20 were used to raise scenery on platforms measuring 4 by 5m/12 by 15ft. The capstans worked on the same basic principles as those used in Nelson's navy 1,800 years later but the labour required must have been even more arduous in the confined and airless tunnels beneath the arena. Even at their fastest, these lifts must have been very slow by modern standards.

The lifts, with human muscle power at times assisted by an ingenious system of counter-weights, carried the caged animals up to just beneath the arena's floor. The beasts were then driven out of the cages on the lifts and up ramps by attendants armed with sticks. They would have emerged, bedazzled, blinking and snarling, into the arena via trapdoors that sprang open suddenly, surprising both spectators and animals. These spring-doors operated on jack-in-the-box principles, flipping open easily but being closed with more effort.

Four larger lifts took bigger creatures such as lions but really massive animals, such as rhinos and elephants, would have been far too heavy. They made their thunderous entrances at ground level, as, albeit more quietly, did the human contestants. All the cages, capstans and lifts were made of wood, so any reconstruction remains conjectural.

NAUMACHIA

It is still uncertain how often – if ever – *naumachia* were held in the Colosseum. *Naumachia* were large-scale, expensive affairs involving scores, even hundreds, of ships and thousands of fighters. (The fighters were all untrained *damnati*, men condemned to death, not proper gladiators.)

▲ *A fanciful Renaissance reconstruction of the* naumachia *(mock sea battles) that Augustus staged in a specially built stadium in Trastevere near the River Tiber. How far this inspired actual* naumachia *inside the Colosseum in its early days remains highly debatable. (Getty)*

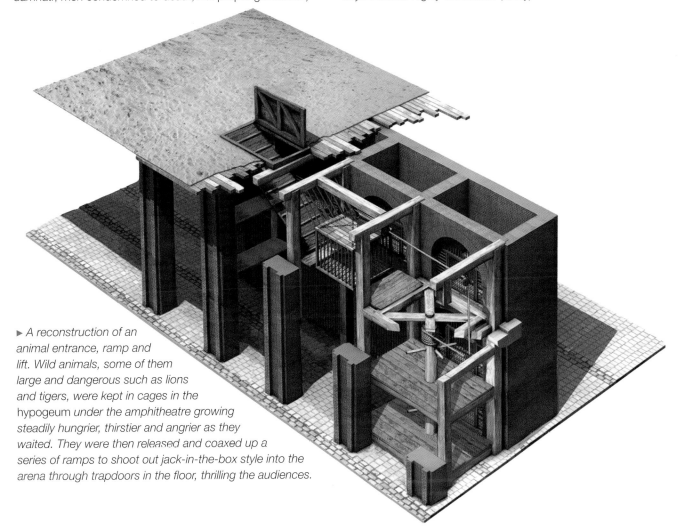

▶ *A reconstruction of an animal entrance, ramp and lift. Wild animals, some of them large and dangerous such as lions and tigers, were kept in cages in the* hypogeum *under the amphitheatre growing steadily hungrier, thirstier and angrier as they waited. They were then released and coaxed up a series of ramps to shoot out jack-in-the-box style into the arena through trapdoors in the floor, thrilling the audiences.*

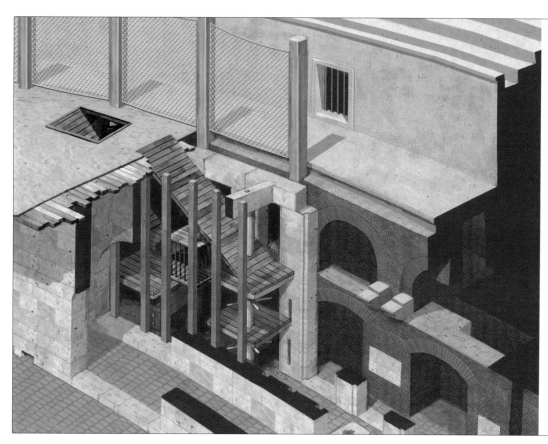

◄ A reconstruc-
tion of the ramp
that ejected wild
animals into the
actual arena
through a sprung
trapdoor. Note
the high net
behind that
protected
spectators both
from enraged
animals and
from any errant
gladiators.

Whether or not *naumachia* were frequently staged in the markedly limited space of the Colosseum, there was certainly a tradition of such contests. Julius Caesar, Augustus and Claudius had hosted *naumachia* in specially dug lakes near the Tiber. Nero held one inside the wooden amphitheatre he had built near the Campus Martius in AD57, so they were clearly not impossible, at least on a small scale. 'He staged a naval battle on an artificial lake of salt water with sea monsters swimming in it,' wrote Suetonius 60 years after the event.

Martial praised a *naumachia* at Titus's inaugural games in the Colosseum in AD80. So did Cassius Dio, writing in CAD220: 'Titus suddenly filled the arena with water and brought in horses and other domesticated animals that had been taught to swim', before describing the same emperor staging a reconstruction of a historical battle between Corcyra (Corfu) and Athens. The galleys involved must have been much smaller than real warships.

Dio also states that Domitian staged a *naumachia* in the

◄ Whether sea
battles ever
occurred inside
the Colosseum is
unclear, but this
reconstruction of
the fan-shaped
area at the
eastern side of
the basement
shows how
galleys could
have been
housed before
such naumachia.

▶ *A fresco from Pompeii showing the riot in its amphitheatre in* AD*59 that led to its temporary closure. It also gives the only illustration of a velarium or awning hoisted above an arena, like a ship's sails. The Colosseum itself may have been too large for such a nautical technique, however. (Getty)*

Colosseum in AD85 but gives no details. If Domitian did, this must have been about the last *naumachia* held there. Once work on the *hypogeum* started, it would have been almost impossible to protect the underground system fully from water.

Dr Beste in his extensive surveys of the *hypogeum* discovered firm evidence that the lower parts of some of the arena's original perimeter wall were once waterproofed with *opus signinum*, the plaster-like cement the Romans used for waterproofing. There is a fan-shaped area at the eastern end of the basement from which scaled-down galleys could have been launched. There are four unusually large conduits that might have been used to flood the arena too, so *naumachia* would have been possible.

Dr Beste in fact calls this very early stage in the Colosseum's existence the 'naumachia period', but he thinks that flooding the arena could never have been quick or easy. Other archaeologists disagree, thinking it could have been flooded and drained in only 30 minutes. Emptying it might have proved easier than filling it, as the existing drainage conduits slope outwards, to take rainwater *out* of the arena.

Whatever the situation initially, it is clear that, when the full-scale *hypogeum* was built under Domitian, flooding the arena must have become impracticable. After the Flavian dynasty, *naumachia* seem to have declined in popularity anyway.

ABOVE THE SPECTATORS: THE VELARIUM
High above the open *cavea* stretched the *velarium*, a giant canvas awning. Spanning most of the *cavea*, with a large gap in the centre to let light in and hot air out, it offered

spectators some protection from the sun and rain. How this shade exactly worked remains something of a mystery. A wall painting from the amphitheatre at Pompeii shows a *velarium* that appears to be supported by yardarms, much like sails on a ship. But it seems unlikely that this nautical approach would have worked for a *cavea* as large as the Colosseum. Around the top part of the amphitheatre's facade are 240 projecting brackets. It is thought that masts inserted through rectangular holes in the cornice rested on these brackets. (The posts on the outer edge of the external pavement around the Colosseum almost certainly had nothing to do with the cables controlling the *velarium*.) Rigging to control the *velarium* was attached to these high brackets, and was operated by sailors

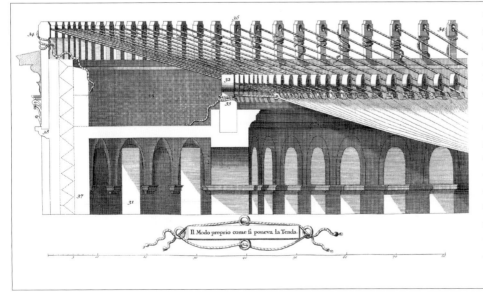

◀ *The* velarium *that covered most of the arena, sheltering spectators from the rain and sun. This line engraving by the Swiss-Italian architect Carlo Fontana in his book* L'Antifeatro Flavio *of 1725 creates a complex system of ropes and masts – originally operated by 1,000 marines – more completely and convincingly than any other drawing. However, as all the amphitheatre's ropes and canvas have long vanished, his work remains conjectural. (Alamy)*

from the regular fleets at Ravenna and Misenum. Around 1,000 marines would have been needed to raise and lower the awnings. Their presence would also have discouraged public disorders, although there are no records of any.

An attempt to reconstruct the *velarium* a few years ago had no success, perhaps because the reconstruction only covered a small part of the arena. The original canvas and ropes have all long vanished and, as happens frustratingly often with ancient technology, contemporary writers did not mention such technical details.

CONSTRUCTION METHODS

Although the architects' overall design of the Colosseum was complex, its execution by teams of workers was facilitated by the use of standardised Roman units and measurements. The ideal ratio of length to width for an arena was 5:3 but a great amphitheatre needed an imposingly grand number of entrance arches. Such arches were traditionally 20 Roman feet wide (a Roman foot equals 296m, almost a modern foot). The Colosseum has 80 arches, an unusual number which meant altering the perimeter size to 1,835 Roman

feet (558m/1,830ft) to take the flanking columns' width into account. The overall external axes were 188 by 166m/556 by 548ft. The size of the auditorium – and so the number of spectators – was left unchanged but the arena was reduced to 280 by 168 Roman feet (83m by 50m/272 by 164ft). This meant that the size of the actual arena, at 3,357sq m/36,134 sq ft, was a little smaller than might be expected for the amphitheatre's overall size.

Working to these well-known ratios, the foremen and craftsmen creating the Colosseum would not have needed constant monitoring by the architects or engineers to create an aesthetically and structurally coherent building. Although the external arches vary a little in detail, reflecting the skills and even tastes of individual workers, overall they are consistent. Importantly, the voussoirs – wedge-shaped stones in the arches essential to support the whole structure – are almost identical throughout.

The outermost annular corridor on the entrance floor is 5m/16ft 6in wide and varies around the entire circumference by less than 1% in width. Clearly the architects could rely upon their vast workforce.

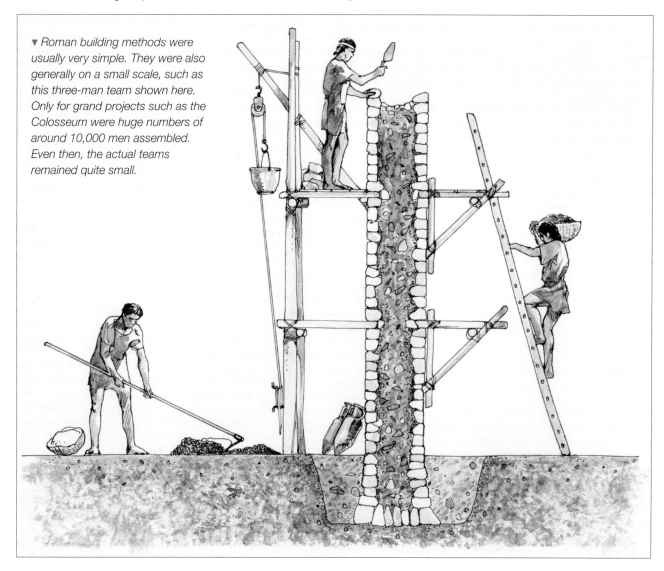

▼ *Roman building methods were usually very simple. They were also generally on a small scale, such as this three-man team shown here. Only for grand projects such as the Colosseum were huge numbers of around 10,000 men assembled. Even then, the actual teams remained quite small.*

MECHANICAL DEVICES: PULLEYS, CRANES, AND WINCHES

While the Romans did not have steam or electrical power, they developed a few ingenious mechanical devices to magnify the human or animal muscle power at their disposal. (They also became masters at utilising waterpower, but this was of no direct help when erecting the Colosseum.) These 'machines' took the form of pulleys, cranes and winches. While on a small scale and very simple by modern standards, they facilitated the rapid building of the Colosseum and the similar grand construction projects that followed.

A good illustration of Roman building techniques in action comes from the tomb of the Haterii. Dating from around AD100 – soon after the Colosseum had been completed – this fine example of Roman sculptural realism also inadvertently reveals a bit of Roman technology. The Haterii, a successful family firm of builders, who could clearly afford a flamboyant burial place, are depicted in carvings on the tomb using a large crane powered by men turning a vast 'squirrel cage'. (A squirrel cage in building purposes is a huge treadmill inside which workers – probably all slaves in ancient Rome – ran up one side, so turning it and the series of connected cables that raised platforms upwards. See illustration.) With such mechanical devices as this it is estimated they could lift marble blocks up to 6m/19ft 6in long. There were probably other such labour-saving devices that have gone unrecorded. This was an area that ancient writers generally ignored, for manual labour was not considered worth mentioning in ancient culture.

> If you are coming from far away and seeing a Roman *munus* for the first time, you should know that this water so like the sea with a naval battle raging on it was until very recently dry land. Don't believe it? Watch while the waters fill with warships. It will happen so fast that you will cry: But only a moment ago there was nothing here but water.
>
> Martial, *Liber de Spectaculis*

▶ *Carving from the Tomb of the Haterii, CAD100. The Haterii were a family of builders who flourished in the Flavian period and were almost certainly involved in the construction of the Colosseum. The near certainty comes from the appearance on their flamboyant tomb of a carving showing what must be the main triumphal entrance arch into the amphitheatre topped by a quadriga. (This is our only surviving visual record of that grand four-horse and chariot sculpture.) Here, however, the focus of interest is less on the building, which is presumably an unknown temple, than on the machinery being used to build it. This is a huge 'squirrel cage', a giant wheel inside which slaves ran up one side, turning it and so via a series of cables lifting the platform to let builders work on the roof. There are no written records of such contraptions and nothing has so far been found by archaeologists, so the tomb provides a very rare glimpse of what was probably a widely used technique. Originally the Haterii may have been freedmen, slaves given their freedom who then became successful businessmen. Certainly the Haterii did not come from the Roman elite, who always spurned practical aspects of life like the building trade. (Alamy)*

3

THE GREAT GAMES

ORIGINS OF THE MUNERA

Gladitorial games were classified as *munera*, the root of the English term 'munifience', public works provided for the Roman people by individuals of high status and wealth. They were as central to the Roman way of life as athletic contests were to the ancient Greeks. Wherever they settled in the empire, the Romans built arenas for their sport. No amphitheatre, however, ever rivalled the Colosseum, the largest, most glamorous and most sophisticated arena in the empire. Beneath the arena's floor lay the two floors of the *hypogeum*, a complex of tunnels and trapdoors where thousands laboured to allow the great shows above their heads to go on.

In the sunlit *cavea* of the amphitheatre, emperors for centuries put on shows of astonishing lavishness, efficiency, splendour and brutality. In some ways they were intended to proclaim the *virtus* (strength, power, courage, manhood) of the Roman Empire itself. Huge resources and organisational skills were deployed with quasi-military efficiency to provide entertainment for just a few days. Almost every day of the games ended in the mass slaughter of both human beings and animals.

This endlessly repeated imperial munificence was designed to impress the people of Rome with their emperor's generosity and regard for them. It was also intended to reassure citizens that, despite no longer having any political power under the new imperial regime, the *populus Romanus* (the Roman people) was still of supreme importance in Rome, the city that was at the centre of the empire and so of the known world.

The varied games around the city were called collectively *circenses*. These included chariot races, the one other spectacle in Rome that rivalled gladiatorial games in splendour and thrills. Chariot races, run by teams who enjoyed the same fanatical fan bases as modern football clubs, were usually held in the vast Circus Maximus, which had the space for them – the Colosseum's arena was too small. The games for which the Colosseum was designed, and is best known for, were the *munera,* meaning the bloody contest of gladiators, and *venationes*, the wild beast fights. *Naumachia*, mock sea battles – though there was nothing

▶ *A re-enactment of a* naumachia*, but on dry land, in the Roman amphitheatre at Nîmes in southern France. (Alamy)*

▲ *Two gladiators, a* retiarius *on the right and (probably) a* secutor *or heavily armed swordsman on the left. (Alamy)*

▼ *Here in the heart of Rome early munera were staged in specially built wooden arenas that were then demolished.*

mock about the deaths of the combatants involved – may have at times been held in the Colosseum also. All are now indelibly associated with our ideas of ancient Rome, and as Juvenal said:

> *Duas tantum res anxius optat/Panem et circenses.*
> (The populace longs for just two things: bread and games)
> Juvenal, *Satire X*, AD100

MUNERA IN ROME

The earliest recorded *munus* (gladiatorial combat) in Rome was held in 264BC, when three pairs of gladiators fought to the death in the Forum Boarium (cattle market) at the funeral of Junius Brutus Pera, a former consul. That this was just before the start of the Punic Wars, the first of the many conflicts that made Rome ruler of the Mediterranean world, is no coincidence. Wars supplied Rome with captives and booty to fund its hugely expensive games. The Colosseum itself was built in part with *manubiae* (war spoils) from the sack of Jerusalem in AD70.

Rome's endless wars had obvious parallels in gladiators' paramilitary combats. A few gladiators even won their freedom by fighting as soldiers, as happened in AD167 when a sudden barbarian invasion threatened the empire. But the origins of the *munus* were religious rather than military. And, as with so many things in Rome, they were not really Roman at all.

ETRUSCAN FUNERALS

The *munus* seems to have originated with the Etruscans, an enigmatic people who influenced the early Romans in many ways. The Etruscans long dominated central Italy, even perhaps ruling Rome itself in the 6th century BC. They also had outposts in the south where they mingled with native Italian peoples such as the Oscans and Samnites and with Greek settlers. Murals from tombs of *c*500BC in the southern city of Paestum show gladiatorial combats that look very like funerary rites.

Munus means 'offering' in a religious sense. *Munera* were originally – and for long afterwards in theory – staged as sacrifices to the gods and the spirits of illustrious dead ancestors, not as sports or entertainment. (*Munus* also had the secondary meaning of payment of due debts.)

FROM FUNERAL RITES TO ELECTORAL BRIBES

In the final two centuries of the Republic up until 31BC, as Rome acquired an empire and ever-growing wealth, gladiatorial games were held with increasing frequency and lavishness. By 216BC the number of fighters at a single event had risen to 22. In 215BC the *munus* given in honour of Aemilius Lepidus involved 22 pairs of gladiators and required the Forum Romanum, the city's principal public place, as its venue. In 174BC, when Quinctius Flaminius, conqueror of Greece, hosted games in honour of his dead father, 74 pairs of men fought each other in contests lasting three days. Evidently the *munus* had already become a form of conspicuous consumption, displaying a family's wealth and status.

Much the grandest *munus* hosted by a Roman noble in the Republic's last years was that given by Julius Caesar to honour his dead father in 65BC: 640 gladiators took part in events over 15 days. Caesar's father had by then been dead for 20 years, highlighting the fact that giving a *munus* now had much less to do with honouring the dead than bribing the electorate in the annual elections for magistrates such as consuls. In Caesar's case this clearly worked, for he was duly later elected consul. The Senate, urged on by the stalwart Republican Cicero, became so alarmed by Caesar's ambitions that it passed laws restricting the size of games to prevent the people being bribed – in vain, as it turned out.

The games Caesar gave to celebrate four triumphs in total – in Gaul, Egypt, Africa and Pontus (northern Anatolia) – in 46BC must have eclipsed those of 65BC but almost no details about them survive. These games did, however, include a *naumachia* staged in a man-made lake near the Tiber, with 6,000 *naumacharii* (mock-sailors). By that date Caesar had made himself dictator for life and the Republic in truth was dead. Two years later Caesar himself was assassinated but his death led only to fresh civil wars, not a restoration of the Republic. After 31BC, when Caesar's (adopted) son Octavius became sole ruler of the Roman world and took the title Augustus – effectively, emperor – he also took control of the games. From now on only the emperor would host the games, getting the kudos of being the sole *editor*.

While Augustus monopolised real power, he was keen to maintain the façade of the Republic, letting the Senate retain many administrative functions. He also wanted to impress the Roman people so that they would see him as their sole benefactor. Rather than building a grand palace like an oriental king, he contented himself with a relatively modest house. Instead he spent money on games, especially *munera*. As the empire lasted nearly five centuries after he had assumed power, he might have thought it money well spent, although Tertullian, a Christian from Carthage, would not:

> Offerings to appease the dead counted as funeral rites and were called a *munus*, being a service due the dead… The ancients thought that by this spectacle they honoured the dead, tempering it [the killing] with a more sophisticated sort of cruelty. For in the past, believing that the souls of the dead are appeased with human blood, they sacrificed captives or slaves who were worth little at funerals. Afterwards, they preferred to disguise this ungodly process by making it into a pleasure. So, after the persons thus procured had been trained – for the sole purpose of learning how to be killed – in the use of such arms as they then had and as well as they could, they then exposed them to death at the tombs on the day appointed for sacrifices in honour of the dead. So they found consolation for death in murder.
>
> Tertullian, *De Spectaculis* ('On the Games'), cAD210

▶ *Gladiatorial contests, originated in funerary games such as these shown on the base of an Etruscan tomb. The Etruscans probably pioneered staging* munera *at funerals as offerings to the god, although on a very small scale. (Alamy)*

THE RULES OF THE GAMES

There was never an official handbook or guide for the games, but even in the remoter provinces of the empire they are thought to have followed much the same procedure after the Colosseum was opened in AD80. This was not a coincidence. The empire's supreme amphitheatre inspired other arenas not just architecturally but in the games themselves. The Colosseum became in effect a guide for other arenas.

Large gladiatorial games were usually advertised in advance of the event. Details of upcoming fights, written in different coloured inks, were posted on walls all round the city, even on tombstones along the main roads into Rome. Two stones found outside Pompeii – the buried city has many of the best surviving artefacts from the arena, thanks to Vesuvius's eruption – announce games at the nearby towns of Nola and Noceram, declaring that the 'whole world loves Numerius Festus Ampliatus's troop of gladiators.' Another inscription from the reign of Claudius (AD41–54) promises: 'Twenty pairs of gladiators provided by Decimus Lucretius Satrius Valens…

and ten pairs of gladiators provided by his son Decimus Lucretrius Valens will fight at Pompeii on 8, 9, 10, 11 and 12 April. There will be a big *venatio* [hunt] and also awnings.' All of which shows that, outside Rome itself, prominent local grandees continued to give such games.

League tables were published so that people could place bets on their favourite gladiators, as they do today with racing horses or football teams. On the night before the first day of the games, the *editor* gave a *cena libera,* a free dinner – free in the sense that the invitees, all of them participants in the events the next day, could eat and drink as much as they liked. The food and wine served were unusually good. Gladiators ate what might just be their last meal – it would be for some but not most – in public, even at times in the Forum, with tables set in the open. Citizens could now observe the gladiators close-up and place further bets. Some gladiators used to get very drunk on these occasions, most notably the wild Celts and Thracians. Others, such as those from the more civilised Greek parts of the empire, might spend the evening making their wills.

▼ *The Roman amphitheatre at Deva Victrix (Chester), as it probably looked in its prime around AD100. The largest amphitheatre in Roman Britain, the stone structure could have seated at least 8,000 people. Archaeological evidence from excavations inside it – only about half of the amphitheatre has been uncovered – suggest that it was used for cock fighting, bull baiting, boxing and wrestling and, most importantly, gladiatorial combats. (Getty)*

▲ *Terracotta figures of a Thracian and a* hoplomachus. *Both these gladiators had small shields. The Thracian's (right) was rectangular, the* hoplomachus's *was round. (Alamy)*

POMPA: THE OPENING CEREMONY

Games started in the morning, when the sun had risen sufficiently to light up the whole *cavea* beneath the *velarium* that protected spectators from the elements. (In the city, not only is the Roman sun fierce, but it can rain suddenly and heavily.) Into the freshly swept arena through the tunnel from the Ludus Magnus (the gladiatorial training school) came the *pompa,* the grand procession of the gladiators. From the massed tiers of the spectators rose the *acclamatio* (applause). If the games were put on by someone other than the emperor, the *pompa* would be headed by the *editor* giving the show. For major events at the Colosseum, however, the emperor was almost always the *editor* (he alone could afford the huge cost) and except for half-mad emperors like Commodus, they always watched the *pompa* from special designated seating on the *podium* as it was thought beneath the imperial dignity to appear in the arena.

ENTRANCE OF THE GLADIATORS

Heading the procession of fighters came the veteran gladiators, riding in chariots. The victors of many games, they made a suitably splendid sight with purple cloaks embroidered with gold and silver thread, bejewelled swords and helmets with ostrich or peacock plumes. Dismounting, they marched around the arena, followed by slaves carrying their arms and armour. These could be equally splendid. Julius Caesar at one *munus* gave 300 of his fighters weapons plated in silver, which must have been more impressive to look at than to use. The tradition long continued. Fabulously decorated weapons have been found dating to the reign of the emperor Commodus (AD180–192), the games-mad emperor.

Now the great day was here and the people had assembled to see our [the gladiators'] suffering. Now 'those about to die' had to lead the procession for their own deaths. The *munerarius*, who was about to win public favour at the cost of our blood, finally took his seat. One thing made me especially miserable: that I seemed so poorly prepared. I was certainly predestined to be a victim in the arena, for no gladiator had cost the munerarius less in training. The whole arena resounded with the apparatus of death. One man was sharpening a sword, another was heating metal in a fire, some gladiators were being beaten with rods, others were scourged with whips [to encourage the reluctant to fight]… Trumpets blared with their funereal sound [trumpets were used at Roman funerals], stretchers were brought in and there was a funeral procession before those carried out were even dead. Everywhere there were wounds, moans, gore…

From a Roman schoolboy's exercise book, CAD100

Reaching the emperor's box, the gladiators lifted their right arms towards him and cried: *Ave Caesar, morituri te salutant!* (Hail Caesar: Those about to die salute you!) Or so the tradition goes. Our only real evidence for this doomed salute comes from Suetonius's description, written some 70 years later, of a *naumachia* on the Fucine Lake given by Claudius in AD52. The inept emperor then reputedly quipped: *Or not!* The fighters joyfully took this as an imperial pardon and laid down their arms until an irate Claudius, hobbling down to the lakeside, managed to coax them to start fighting. These *naumacharii* would all have been criminals condemned to die while entertaining the Roman people, but in this case many were apparently pardoned, something unusual for a *naumachia*. In a normal *munus* real gladiators, whose training made them very expensive performers, did not all die, so the salute would have been inappropriate.

MUSICAL ACCOMPANIMENTS

Music played an important ancillary part in the day's events. It was performed mainly during the *pompa* and probably also later to announce each new act and in the intervals, when the arena was being cleared of blood and bodies. Wind instruments, chiefly brass and especially the *tuba*, the Roman army's war-trumpet, along with pipes and flutes, predominated, but there was also a mobile hydraulic organ. At times the organ was played by female organists, at least according to evidence from mosaics. This was one of the rare occasions when women appeared in the arena. Singers also contributed to the music, which was likely to have been martial and exciting, although the music itself remains unknown. The music heightened the drama and tension, as it does in films.

VENATIONES: THE MORNING HUNT

Venationes, animal hunts, date back at least as far as 169BC, when a fight involving 63 leopards, 40 bears and an unknown number of elephants was held in the Circus Maximus. Until shortly before the Colosseum was built, gladiatorial fights and *venationes* were usually staged on separate occasions. But by AD80 *venationes* had joined the *munus* proper as part of an all-day event. By then the *venatio* had become established as the first real event of the day. The name of the school for these performers, the Ludus Matutinus (the 'morning' school) established in Rome at just about this time, reveals that they were indeed the morning act.

The *venationes* and *munus* had much in common. Both were violent combats that could end in death for either opponent, but in both the lives of any of the contestants, even the animals, might be spared because of their courage. Knowledge of this was a powerful incentive to human contestants. Some of the animals shown on mosaics of *venationes* have names, suggesting that they survived enough fights to be recognised, even cherished, as individuals by spectators. Names of animals found on mosaics near El Djem in Tunisia include Victor, Crudelis (cruel) and Omicida (man-killer).

▼ *A 4th-century AD mosaic from Villa Piazza Armerina, Sicily, showing a lion attacking a* venator *(hunter).*

The original meaning of *venatio* was hunting in the wild but it came to mean equally 'hunting' in the arena. There were two sorts of hunters: *venatores* and *bestiarii*. The events of the day focused on *venatores*, hunters trying to kill animals of many sorts, especially exotic beasts such as lions, tigers, leopards, rhinos, hippos, bears and elephants. *Venatores* wore a short tunic and were armed with a light spear and a small shield, as they may have been when hunting in the wild.

The *bestiarius*, by contrast, was a heavily armed figure, with a sword, shield and helmet, naked from the waist up like a gladiator. Originally *bestiarii* may have been gladiators transferred to take part in the *venatio*. Some are thought to have served as assistants to *venatores*, others to have slaughtered animals on their own. By AD100 they became less common.

▲ *Tigers for the arena were then found across western Asia, in what is now Turkey, and northern Iran.*

LEAPING INTO THE ARENA

Both types of fighter always faced the sudden threat of animals being sprung on them – literally. Wolves, tigers, lions and leopards would leap from trapdoors in the arena's floor behind the fighters. The element of surprise – which could lead to the fighter being mauled if not killed – added greatly to the morning's thrills. The cages that brought the animals up into the arena were winched up in 32 lifts powered by men turning capstans from the *hypogeum* below. The entrances of the heavier animals – bears, bulls, hippos, rhinos and

especially elephants – could not be shot into the arena through these trapdoors. They were also far too heavy for these small lifts. But, as they thundered into the arena from one of the hidden gates at ground level, their entrances must have been almost as dramatic.

One potential problem with any *venatio* was getting the animals actually to fight. After being kept in the dark of the *hypogeum* for hours before being thrust into the sunlit arena's glare, some animals, bedazzled and bewildered, tried to slink into the shade. There they would have been nearly invisible to many spectators. To avoid such unsporting behaviour, the arena's shady side – the eastern and southern sides during the morning hunts – was at times barricaded off, forcing the animals into the sunlit centre of the arena.

Although kept hungry and thirsty to increase their savagery, some animals still needed to be goaded to make them attack humans or other beasts. A *pila* (ball) or a stuffed dummy of their normal prey might be thrown at them. Once the games were well under way, the smell of freshly spilt blood proved as arousing to carnivorous animals as it was to human onlookers. The herbivores, the prey of the great cats, bears and wolves, would have shown signs of terror, which was

▼ *This mosaic from Villa Piazza Armerina shows the elaborate techniques involved in finding, trapping and transporting wild animals in Africa for the arena. The ox cart in the foreground ferried caged beasts to the waiting ships.*

▲ A leopard leaps onto an antelope desperately trying to escape. Such scenes of feral savagery were frequently re-enacted in the arena, delighting the sadistic Roman audience.

◀ A quadriga, a four-horse chariot, the horses sporting festive headwear. Chariots never raced in the Colosseum but they often paraded around before games started.

very gratifying to the audience. Few written details have been left of the *venationes* themselves, so we have to rely mainly on murals and mosaics. Fortunately, we have these in abundance right down to the 4th century AD, with the mosaics from the villa at Piazza Armerina in Sicily.

Roman audiences loved to see illusionistic scenery in the theatre or amphitheatre, the more elaborate and realistic the better. Trees with all their branches and leaves would pop up in the arena to represent woods, while wooden rocks would stand in for mountains. This created an instant wilderness inside the city. While genuine hunting was the exclusive preserve of the Roman aristocracy, the people of Rome, who lived all year in crowded *insulae* (tenement blocks) in the world's most densely populated city, could enjoy a substitute for country life watching the hunting in the *venatio*. Fights between animals seldom pitted one creature against another

◀ Hunting enactments didn't always end well for the human participants, here, one has been gored by a huge wild boar.

HUNTED TO EXTINCTION

Supplying the games required trapping wild animals and then transporting them perhaps thousands of miles by land and sea to Rome. Carnivores like lions would be lured by tethered sheep or goats to traps in the ground. They would then be netted and carried away in carts, a tricky business without tranquillising drugs. The process must have required not only genuine hunting skills from real *venatores* but diligence in taking care of the beasts. Mosaics from Piazza Armerina in Sicily, dating from c AD310, show the animals being carefully loaded on to ships for transport to Rome. The mortality rate must have been high, which in turn required even more animals to be caught, a process that in the long term proved disastrous.

In the first millennium BC lions, tigers, leopards and panthers still roamed freely across western Asia and North Africa. Although hunted at times by the kings of Assyria and Persia, they managed to survive, even thrive, in areas that were then less arid and better forested than they are today. On the banks of the river Nile in Egypt there were still

▲ *The Roman people's hunger for brutal thrills demanded that animals from across North Africa, western Asia and Europe be transported to the imperial city. Here animals are being loaded on to ships to be taken to Rome.*

hippos and rhinos while lions, ostriches and elephants – the smaller, more biddable North African Forest elephant used by Hannibal – were common north of the Sahara. But 500 years of the Romans' rapacious exploitation, which had begun back in the Republic, led to these areas' denudation. In 59 BC Quintus Cicero, who was the younger brother of the great orator and Republican Marcus Cicero, and *propraetor* (governor) of Asia (western

Turkey), was already complaining of the difficulty of procuring enough wild animals to satisfy Roman audiences. Apart from a few lions that long survived in the Atlas Mountains, all such species have now gone extinct in these regions. Only the fauna of northern Europe – bears, bulls, deer, wolves – survived in healthy numbers, due to much of that region remaining outside Roman power.

of the same species. To make contests more unpredictable and exciting, lions would be pitted against tigers – tigers usually won, surprising those who considered the lion king of the beasts – and rhinoceroses against bears or bulls. The rhino, a beast that was often usefully bad-tempered, was normally the victor with both, tossing its unhappy opponents in the air like balls. Bulls and bears were more evenly matched. Rhinos, like elephants and wildcats from Asia and Africa, had great appeal precisely because they were more difficult to obtain than wolves, bears or bulls. Augustus in his *Res Gestae* (Deeds), while boasting that in the 26 *venationes* he had given some 3,500 animals were killed, stressed that many were exotic species such as lions and leopards. Titus easily surpassed this score in his grand inaugural games for the Colosseum in AD80, killing 5,000 animals, while Trajan slaughtered yet more.

Not every animal that appeared in the arena faced certain death. Martial mentions more innocent performances by highly trained animals that sound like circus turns: teams of

panthers obediently drawing chariots, elephants kneeling to trace out Latin phrases in the dust. There could be an element of scientific inquiry, too, as wild animals from the far corners of the then known world captured and brought to Rome were sometimes kept in private zoos. But science was seldom the real reason for an animal's appearance in the Colosseum.

Bears and lions were obvious candidates for *venationes*. So too in their vulnerable way were deer. But the Romans somehow also got large birds such as cranes and ostriches to fight – or at least to die – entertainingly in the arena. These birds, like deer, must have been released in the same jack-in-the-box way as leopards or lions. Cassius Dio mentions fights being staged between elephants and cranes, although how these creatures were persuaded to fight each other is unknown. To spice up the display even further, some *editores* took to dying animals' fur and feathers strange colours, such as purple and silver. This may have gone down well with the populace, but was considered excessively vulgar by the inevitably upper class commentators.

THE NOONDAY SPECTACLE

Around noon, the wealthier members of the audience, especially senators in their reserved front-row seats, would leave the Colosseum for a lunch break and a siesta. This was the usual time for the *meridianum spectaculum*, the noonday spectacle of public executions of *damnati* (condemned criminals), a custom institutionalised under the emperor Claudius who had a taste for such things. Some light entertainment seems to have been given first in the form of the *pegniarii*, play-gladiators who amused the crowd by fighting each other with wooden weapons and whips.

EXECUTIONS AS ENTERTAINMENT

Plenty of offences were punishable by death in ancient Rome, among them desertion from the army, counterfeiting, poisoning, parricide, kidnapping, treason, treachery, practising magic, atheism and following a banned religion. The last two offences could catch out Christians. As Christians often gathered in secrecy for their services, ostentatiously rejected all other deities and refused to take part in emperor-worship – which was more like swearing loyalty to the flag than literal worship – they appeared abominably treacherous to most people in the polytheistic empire.

If convicted of a capital offence, aristocratic Romans could expect a swift and dignified death, normally by

▼ *A* damnatus *(condemned man) being mauled to a death by a lion. Such public executions were popular with the people, but the elite deplored the lack of skill involved. (Getty)*

beheading. (Although many in fact went into exile.) But citizens of the lower class, who by the year AD150 were being classified as *inferiores* (inferiors), and non-citizens and slaves faced far worse fates. Roman ingenuity transformed their mass executions into forms of entertainment. The upper classes tended to scorn such spectacles, not because of the cruelty but because of the lack of skill involved. No such snobbery prevented poorer Romans from enjoying them – and anyway, they dared not leave their unmarked seats for fear of losing them.

Death by beast

Damnatio ad bestias (condemnation to the wild animals) was considered a most exciting form of public death for spectators, more so than simple crucifixion, which could be tediously long. Although a little resistance by the *damnati* was often encouraged – they might be given inadequate weapons to fight each other or the wild beasts, so prolonging both their agony and the spectacle – there was almost no chance of reprieve. *Damnatio* meant inescapably execution, as in more recent times did death by hanging, the electric chair or guillotine. The *damnati* included war captives such as the 2,500 Jews reputedly killed in the arena of Caesarea in Palestine at Titus's triumph in AD70. (This figure comes from the writings of Titus's protégé Josephus, who habitually exaggerated.) Constantine, the first Christian emperor, hosted

> The proconsul [provincial governor] has to decide the penalty for robbing a temple. This will depend on the social status of the person concerned, the circumstances surrounding the affair and the offender's age and sex, the penalty being adjusted to make it more severe or more merciful. I know that many proconsuls have condemned temple-robbers to *damnatio ad bestias*. But others have had such robbers burnt alive while others have had the robbers hanged. The penalty should always be *damnatio ad bestias* for those who have broken into a temple at night as members of an organised gang and carried off valuable items donated to the god. But if a person stole something only of lesser value during the daytime, the penalty should be labour in the mines.
>
> *Ulpian*, Edicts, CAD220

▲ *A 19th-century view of Nero's persecution of the Christians in AD64. Many were nailed to crosses and burnt alive – in the Circus Maximus, not in the as yet unbuilt Colosseum. (Getty)*

events in which German war captives had to fight each other to the death to entertain his troops in Gaul.

The *damnati* were often lashed to stakes and then exposed to wild animals. Sometimes, as mosaics from Zliten in Tunisia show, men were tied to carts that were pushed in front of wild cats who clawed them to shreds. The audience jeered at the blood streaming down the victims' bodies, joking that the *damnati* were at last having a good shower.

Human torches

Burning people alive had even greater popular appeal. The *damnati* so chosen were called *pyrriarchi* and dressed in costumes soaked in inflammable liquids. When these were ignited, they had to dance until they dropped dead.

Nero famously scapegoated the Christians for the Great Fire that gutted most of Rome in AD64, partly to deflect suspicions that he had started the blaze. He had some Christians coated in pitch and lit as living torches to illuminate his novel night-time games in the Circus Maximus. This proved too much even for Roman tastes, as Tacitus writes:

> Some were covered with skins of wild beasts and left to be devoured by dogs; others were nailed to crosses; many were burnt alive and many covered in inflammable matter and lighted to serve as torches at night.
>
> Tacitus, *Annals,* CAD110,

ANDROCLES AND THE LION

Not every encounter between human and animal in the arena was fatal. Whether or not true, the famous tale of Androcles and the Lion is a venerable story, coming down to us via the Roman author Aulus Gellius (CAD123–165) from a lost work by Apion, an earlier Hellenistic writer. Androcles was a runaway slave who was recaptured and sentenced by his master to *damnatio ad bestias*, a common punishment for such escapees. Thrown into the arena to be devoured by lions, he was instead greeted by a lion that purred and licked his feet, to universal surprise. The emperor Augustus, the *editor*, was so intrigued that he halted the event and asked Androcles to explain. Androcles told him that he had escaped a cruel master in North Africa by fleeing into the desert, where he lived like a hermit in a cave. One day he encountered a lion that was limping painfully. Androcles, seeing what was the matter, extracted a large thorn from the animal's paw, so earning his undying gratitude. The two lived together until Androcles decided to return to civilisation, which led to his recapture. The lion was also caught and sent to Rome. Charmed by the tale and backed by the crowd, Augustus, who always liked to grant *missio* (mercy), pardoned both Androcles and his lion. Later, man and lion were to be seen walking happily around Rome together, with the lion on a lead.

MARTYRS IN THE COLOSSEUM: FACT OR FICTION?

Pope Benedict XIV's decision in 1749 to dedicate the Colosseum to Jesus and pronounce it sanctified by the blood of martyrs was vital in saving the amphitheatre's structure from further depredations. A large cross had already been erected on the west side of the *cavea*, and regular services were from then on held inside the amphitheatre to commemorate the fates of the holy victims. Each Good Friday the Pope still leads a procession that starts at the Colosseum.

Behind Benedict's intervention was the belief, widespread at the time and still frequently accepted, that the arena had been the site of numerous Christian martyrdoms. Jean-Léon Gérôme, a French 19th-century academic artist, painted the classic image in *The Last Prayer*, a touching scene. But this picture, and the story it illustrates, are based on no more than legends. There is no documentary evidence of *any* Christians being executed for their faith inside Rome's amphitheatre. The one apparent exception, the death of Telemachus in AD404 who leapt into the arena to stop the fighting, hardly counts. Although Telemachus was later canonised, he was

killed accidentally – according to some accounts, by annoyed gladiators – and not officially condemned to death.

Early Christian writers recorded the deaths of martyrs in the various arenas such as Carthage, Arles or Antioch in Syria with meticulous care – they knew the value of publicity. Undoubtedly Christians were killed in the Circus Maximus, the Colosseum's rival as a site for bloody entertainments. The process started with the nameless victims burnt alive when Nero decided to scapegoat Christians after the Great Fire of AD64. St Ignatius of Antioch was martyred in the Circus in AD108, as was carefully recorded. So if there had been similar deaths of saintly celebrities in the Colosseum, they would have surely been noted.

Absence of evidence is not evidence of absence of course. Some Christians – who were often ranked simply as common criminals – probably did meet unrecorded deaths during the noontide sessions of mass execution. One likely reason that Colosseum authorities seldom chose to 'throw Christians to the lions' was that Christians could not be relied upon to

▲ The Christian Martyrs' Last Prayer*, 1863, by Jean-Léon Gérôme. Gérôme created the archetypal image of Christians being martyred in the Colosseum. There is no evidence of this ever occurring however. (Alamy)*

provide good entertainment. Christians would almost never fight back or try to escape, but instead accepted their fates, often while singing hymns or psalms with what must have struck pagan spectators as unsettling joy. (Martyrdom was thought by the early Christians to guarantee a quick passage to heaven.) The Colosseum, as the empire's premier amphitheatre, wanted to stage only first-rate, thrilling shows, a trait not universally approved of:

> Human beings should be sacred to humankind. But nowadays men are killed in games for fun! It was once a crime to teach men how to receive or inflict wounds, but now men are led out into the arena naked and defenceless, simply to provide entertainment by their deaths.
>
> Seneca, Roman philosopher and satirist (c4BC–AD65)

Death as theatre

There is no evidence of any Christians being martyred inside the Colosseum, although during 250 years of intermittent persecutions Christians were killed in other arenas around the empire, most notably in Carthage. Christian writers described in gloating detail these deaths, which they saw as guaranteeing them a place in heaven. It seems likely that any martyrdom in the greatest amphitheatre of all would have been carefully recorded. The martyrdom by *damnatio ad bestias* of St Ignatius of Antioch in AD107 is celebrated, for example, but this took place in the Circus Maximus, not the Colosseum. For most Romans at the time, Christians were simply criminals who had to be executed. Christians could only have made up a small proportion of the *damnati*, being only a small minority of people in the empire until Constantine's conversion, despite the impression that some Christian writers have given.

A common feature of such executions was to turn the death of the *damnati* into dramatic performances, when the convicts had to act out mythological or historical scenes ending with their painful deaths. For example, the myth of Prometheus, who was tied to a rock in the Caucasus and had his liver gnawed each day by an eagle, was somehow re-enacted. So was the myth of Pasiphae, queen of Crete, who became so besotted with a bull that, disguised as a cow, she was impregnated by it. Presumably the condemned women forced into these dramatic recreations died as a result.

On another occasion a *damnato* playing the role of Icarus – in myth the son of Daedalus who flew so close to the sun that his wax wings melted – crashed near the imperial box, spattering the emperor Nero with his blood. Tertullian also mentions victims being forced to re-enact the fate of Attis, the Syrian god who castrated himself, or the Greek hero Hercules who burnt himself to death. These men were often condemned outlaws. The events would all have been staged with great technical brilliance.

It is easy to shudder at the Roman's delight in such cruelty and condemn them as hyper-organised sadists. Unquestionably, Romans loved watching these painful and complex forms of capital punishment but death was omnipresent in the ancient world. Life expectancy was very low, with few of the poorer Romans living beyond 50. The *damnati* were seen as criminals and so Romans believed that they were fully deserving of a painful death. Public executions were intended to act as a warning to other possible malefactors, as was the case in many other societies.

Public executions remained very popular in Britain, attracting crowds of eager onlookers, right up to their abolition in 1868. Public executions had a similar appeal in the USA where they continued even longer, until 1936. As contemporary films and television demonstrate, modern audiences have not lost a taste for brutal violence, albeit it is now simulated. If the *munera* were revived today, they might draw similarly large audiences, probably taking selfies.

THE MAIN EVENT

After the lunchtime break, the Colosseum filled up again for the day's climax: the gladiatorial combats. Not many accounts of what actually happened inside the Colosseum survive. Hollywood has attempted to fill this gap, most recently in Ridley Scott's colourful film *Gladiator* (2000). Although this is generally very accurate in its reconstruction of the actual amphitheatre, it errs with dramatic licence when depicting the contests themselves. These were seldom, if ever, the free-for-all melees included in the film, at which Russell Crowe excelled.

Instead, gladiatorial combat tended to be carefully controlled duels between two selected individual gladiators, normally of different types. A large-scale *munus* might last more than three hours with 12 to 16 matches, each lasting around 15 minutes and supervised by the *lanista*. Some further time must have been allowed to let the *editor* make the needed life and death decisions – ultimately it was up to the *editor* to decide who was going to die and who to live – and for arena attendants, called *harenari* (sand men), to clean up the mess.

▼ *Almost all gladiatorial combats took place between two skilled fighters. Here the man on the left must be a Thracian as he fights with the* sica, *a curved sword. The exact type of the other gladiator is less clear but he could be a* hoplomachus. *(Getty)*

PRE-SHOW ENTERTAINMENT

A *munus* would typically start with a few warm-up acts before the actual fighting. These took the form of 'freak shows' with cripples, dwarfs, men on stilts goading animals, performances by jugglers and acrobats, and other circus-like diversions. At times they re-enacted mythological dramas. Such myths were central to Greco-Roman religion.

The writer Apuleius (born AD123) described one such event in the arena in his romantic novel *The Golden Ass*. Three young women playing Venus, Juno and Minerva re-enact the Judgement of Paris, surrounded by little boys dressed as cupids and girls representing the seasons. As befits the goddess of love, Venus is naked apart from a thin silk smock that the wind blows open. Mercury, the messenger god played by a handsome young man, was

▲ *A gladiator, perhaps a Thracian, is attacked by big cats, probably lions, while his* lanista *looks on. Above, spectators look down from what must be the imperial box. (Alamy)*

also naked apart from his winged helmet and sandals. Young Prince Paris, who by running off with Helen of Troy will trigger the Trojan War, is shown tending goats on a hill. Later in the event a stream ran red to indicate the bloodshed his elopement would cause. As in a *venatio*, elaborate scenery was an important part of the proceedings.

THE PRIME SPECTACLE
All this was a mere taster for the main event. Finally, the sound of trumpets, woodwind and singing announced the arrival of the true masters of the arena through the ceremonial entrance at the western end of the longer axis. After (probably) saluting the emperor, a ritual sharpening of weapons followed, swords being tested in the *probatio armorum* (the testing of the weapons). Officials prepared the whips, canes and heated iron bars to warn any gladiators who failed to fight and ritually beat the *tiros* (novices) to encourage them to fight hard, while *equites* (horsemen) galloped around the arena. When the trumpets sounded, the gladiators retreated to the arena's edge and the *equites* charged towards each other. Their fights soon finished, however, to make way for the next act.

There was probably seldom more than one fight going on at the same time in the arena. Written sources are not clear about this and the evidence from mosaics and murals is muddled. In some, more than one pair of gladiators appears to be fighting simultaneously in the arena, but examination usually reveals that they are the same two men at different stages of their duel. It would have been difficult for the referees to control more than one fight and for the emperor or another *editor* to decide on the victor. Remarkably, the only literary record of an actual fight we have is a poem in Martial's *Liber spectaculorum* praising Titus's inaugural games of AD80. It describes how the champion gladiators Priscus and Verus both fought so well that Titus finally declared them joint winners.

Priscus and Verus seem to have been gladiators of the same type, probably both *murmillo* or *hoplomachus*. But Roman audiences loved contrasts. A common form of combat was that between two very different sorts of fighter: a *retiarius*, a nearly naked net man, and a *secutor*, a heavily armed gladiator whose helmet had very small holes for the eyes. Such a helmet kept the *secutor's* face safe from the *retiarius's* trident but meant that his vision was severely restricted, as was his breathing. This gave the unarmoured *retiarius* his chance. If he could dance around the *secutor*, keeping out of his reach until the latter was exhausted and gasping for breath, the *secutor* could then be entrapped in the net, bringing the fight to an end.

MISSIO – OR TRIUMPH
Most gladiatorial fights did not end in the quick death of one of the contestants in the combat. More often the defeated gladiator, wounded or at the victor's mercy, would raise his left index finger to show that he was beaten and to ask for *missio*. *Missio* means 'release', or 'mercy'. Then the trumpets would sound again and the *lanista* (trainer) parted the two men. It was then up to the *editor* to decide on the defeated gladiator's fate. Before deciding, the *editor* listened carefully to the *vox populi*, the voice of the people resonating in the amphitheatre, and looked to see how people's thumbs were turned. If the people were pleased with the contest, they

would cry *Missus!* and wave their handkerchiefs or clothing. If they thought the defeated gladiator had put up a feeble fight and deserved no mercy, they would cry, *'Habet!'*, ('let him have it') or, *'Lugera!'* ('cut his throat'). Augustus almost always granted *missio,* in line with his official magnanimity, but Caligula and Domitian often refused it. As the poet Juvenal wrote, 'Even a gladiator defeated in the arena continues to hope, although the crowd threatens him with hostile thumbs.' Occasionally it was left to the victorious gladiator to decide – a tricky choice, as the fallen man might well be a friend but the victor would

not wish to disappoint his audience or the emperor. If *missio* was refused, the victor would finish off his opponent very swiftly. Even at this moment the defeated man could make a good impression by bravely offering up his throat to be cut. Then the victor plunged his sword or dagger into his doomed opponent's throat.

A powerful reason for granting *missio* was the expense incurred in training fresh gladiators. Also, even the most brilliant gladiator would suffer the odd defeat, as posters from Pompeii advertising forthcoming displays show. They list men who had

UP OR DOWN?

In Jean-Léon Gérôme's famous 1872 painting *Pollice Verso* ('thumbs turned'), which inspired Ridley Scott's *Gladiator*, a triumphant gladiator turns to see if spectators want him to spare his adversaries, one of whom is a

defeated *retiarius*. Most of the audience have their thumbs turned down, which has been interpreted as indicating that there should be no *missio*. 'Thumbs down' has since come to mean disapproval or rejection. In fact, the scholarly consensus now is that it in ancient Rome it meant the

survived up to 30 fights but only won about half of them. It has been estimated that when the Colosseum was inaugurated and for decades after, only about 20% of defeated gladiators who asked for *missio* were denied it. By the year AD200, however, this proportion seems to have doubled to 40%. Possibly Roman audiences had grown addicted to ever more brutal thrills after the reign of Commodus (AD180–192).

The triumphant gladiator would parade around the arena, receiving the adulation of the crowd sometimes along with flowers and trinkets, before receiving the *palma*, or palm of

victory, from the emperor. If he had fought especially well, the gladiator might also win a crown. The *editor* might also offer a financial reward; audibly counting out the gold coins he gave the victor so that the crowd would yet again applaud his munificence. Gladiators who had a long line of such victories could hope one day to receive the wooden sword of release.

DISPOSAL OF THE DEAD

While the exultant victor was prancing around the arena waving at his fans, the corpses of the defeated had to be disposed of. Two officials, a man dressed as Mercury with a wand, and a figure disguised as Charun, the Etruscan demon of the dead, entered the arena. Mercury would prod each corpse to ensure the gladiator really was dead and not shamming or passed out. If there was any doubt, Charun would dispatch the defeated with his hammer and the corpse would then be dragged out with hooks through the Porta Libitina, the Gate of Execution. If the winner was also wounded, which was often the case, he might be carried on a litter back to the Ludus Magnus to be cared for.

Games over several days produced many dead human bodies and far more animal corpses. What to do with these was a real problem. Poorer people in Rome were often happy to eat bulls and deer killed in the arena. But when the half-mad emperor Caligula tried to have human corpses treated as a source of cheap food, citizens objected vehemently.

Defeated gladiators could not rely on getting a proper funeral unless comrades in the arena or relatives outside arranged the rites. This ceremony was vitally important in Roman religion. The corpses of the far more numerous *damnati* were usually defaced and thrown into mass graves, symbolising their ignominious posthumous fate.

◄ Pollice Verso, *1872, by Jean-Léon Gérôme. Meaning 'thumbs turned', this colourful work shows the dramatic moment when a victorious gladiator asks whether or not to spare his conquered adversary. Architecturally accurate – note the Vestal Virgins on the right, the only women allowed actually near the arena, all thumbing away – it almost certainly misinterprets the actual thumb-turning. Roman spectators turned their thumbs down and away to signify* **missio** *(mercy) and in towards the throat to demand a gladiator's death. The emperor, as* editor, *had the final decision. (Alamy)*

opposite. Thumbs down – or away from the person making the gesture, towards the arena – meant release, while pointing the thumb up, towards the person's own throat, meant no mercy. Gérome's misinterpretation remains widely believed, however.

▼ *Slaves who checked the bodies of the fallen were dressed as Mercury, a link with the funerary origins of the games.*

4

THE GLADIATORS

TRAINING, DEATH, AND FREEDOM?

Gladiators were the superstars of ancient Rome, in some ways resembling footballers today. The fact that gladiators faced the prospect of death each time they appeared in the arena only added to their dangerous glamour. Admired for their fighting skills, they also radiated huge sex appeal, thanks to their half-naked muscular bodies on display in the arena. Some aristocratic Roman women took them as lovers, including reputedly more than one empress, despite deep official disapproval. So great was the lure of the games that at times upper-class men also tried their luck in the arena. This was at times because a despotic emperor such as Nero had ordered them to do so, but more often it was because even a few aristocrats found themselves attracted to the gladiators' potent combination of fame and fortune – or glorious death.

There was a paradox about these celebrity performers, however. Glittering though some gladiators' careers might seem – and a few successful ones could hope to retire fairly rich and very famous – they were recruited overwhelmingly from criminals and other social outcasts called *infames*. A typical punishment for severe offences was *damnatio ad ludum gladiatorum* meaning 'condemned to the gladiatorial games'. A gladiator's social and political status was on a par

▼ *A panoramic view of the arena towards sunset. Most of the* hypogeum *is now exposed to the elements but a small part of the floor has been restored.*

with a prostitute's or pimp's, at the very bottom of a deeply hierarchical society. Legally they were no better than slaves, wholly at the mercy of their master, the *lanista* (trainer). Many had previously been slaves who had been sold into the arena; many others were war captives with no rights at all.

Simultaneously regarded by Romans as a hero and a criminal, a successful gladiator was both an idol of the games-mad public and, in official eyes, something of a pariah. In this he was very unlike ancient Greek athletes, citizens who were celebrated as heroes by their native cities, having statues erected in their honour. In this sense, the gladiator cannot really be compared with modern footballers, those

present-day celebrities who are all free men. A gladiator was in some ways forever tainted by his role.

Although all gladiators lost their rights as Roman citizens, a few desperately poor citizens, *auctorati,* enrolled for a fixed term in exchange for a cash sum. One thing that gladiators from all backgrounds had in common was that they were skilled, tough professionals. They had to be, or they would have not lasted more than a day in the Colosseum. And a fully trained gladiator could hope to survive many games.

Just as Prometheus bound on a Caucasian rock
Fed with his ever regrowing liver
The vulture that never tires of eating, So a man cast as
Laureolus the bandit and nailed to a cross – no stage prop –
Offered his exposed guts to a mountain bear.
His shredded limbs clung to life although
Their varied parts gushed with blood…
Finally he got the punishment he deserved…
Maybe he had cut his master's throat,
Maybe he'd robbed a temple of its gold,
Maybe he had tried to burn our city of Rome…
Through him what had been a myth
Became a real punishment.
Martial, *Liber Spectaculorum* Book II, CAD83

▲ *This is thought to be one of the gladiators' entrances from the Ludus Magnus, their chief school, into the arena.*

▶ Death of a Gladiator, *an engraving by Peyns from a painting by Marco Landuchi, 1888, shows a defeated gladiator's corpse being dragged off while the victor is carried in triumph around the arena.*

GLADIATOR SCHOOLS

By the 1st century BC gladiators were no longer amateurs but were properly trained at special schools, *ludi*. This growing specialism marked the final transition in a gladiator's status from a victim invariably sacrificed at funerary games in a mutually destructive fight, to a highly disciplined and accomplished professional. It echoed the similar transformation of the Roman army from a glorified citizens' militia to the most impressive army the world had yet seen, a process begun by the radical politician Marius in 107BC.

At first all *ludi* were private. The *ludus* at Capua was the largest and also the most professional, housing many hundreds of fighters. Gladiators from Capua long retained a distinct prestige. Similar schools sprang up in Rome – the poet Horace mentions a Ludus Aemilius, which must have been private, as there were no publicly maintained *ludi* at this time. With the Flavian dynasty, Rome's rulers finally established under imperial control the empire's four largest *ludi* in Rome: the Ludus Magnus, 54m/60yd east of the

Colosseum (the largest school for gladiators), the Ludus Matutinus, for *venatores* (the animal fighters), the Ludus Gallicus and the Ludus Dacicus. Very little is known about these two smaller *ludi*, even their exact locations still being uncertain. The Ludus Dacicus must have had a ready supply of gladiators in captives from the Dacian Wars under Domitian and, even more significantly, under Trajan.

The names of some of these gladiatorial schools – Ludus Gallicus, Ludus Dacicus – reveal how the recruitment of fighters for the arena often depended heavily on Rome's wars of conquest. Spartacus, the great rebel gladiator, was despite his name a Thracian, from a part of the southeast

▼ *The excavated ruins of Ludus Magnus – the famous gladiator school that fed Rome's Colosseum with its fighters.*

► *A venator* (hunter) *from a mosaic at Nannig in the Moselle Valley, Germany. Many venatores used tridents such as this rather than swords to fight wild beasts, presumably preferring the greater range and flexibility such a weapon gave. This fine mosaic from* CAD*100 shows how popular gladiatorial themes were as decorative motifs across the empire, and how Romanised locals became. (Alamy)*

Balkans ruthlessly exploited by Rome long before its final absorption into the empire in AD48. Julius Caesar's militarily brilliant conquest of Gaul (today France, the Rhineland and Belgium) from 58 to 51BC led to a depopulation of the area so intense that it approached genocide, and must have provided a flood of recruits for Rome's arenas. Trajan's similarly spectacular conquest of Dacia (today Romania) in AD101–106 provided another rush of slaves, as the carvings on Trajan's column indicate. Some of these captives must have been good gladiator material.

As late as the 4th century AD, when Roman armies had long been on the defensive, emperors such as Constantine I, (reigned AD306–337), or Maximus Magnus, who ruled the Western Empire AD383–388, used German war captives as arena fodder for games at Trier, then Rome's western capital.

▼ *A detail from Trajan's famous column in Rome showing war captives from his Dacian campaign, some of whom ended up fighting in the arena as gladiators.*

▼ *A corridor beneath the amphitheatre at Capua, a wealthy city in southern Italy. Built under Augustus, it is the second-largest amphitheatre in the Roman world.*

▲ *A reconstruction of the Ludus Magnus, Rome's largest training school for gladiators. Built of brick-faced concrete, its courtyard had porticoes around an arena that measured 63m by 43m (69 by 47yd) with seating for 3,000 spectators. Gladiators seldom left the Ludus, except to fight in the arena.*

In practice, some able-bodied young war captives may have welcomed the chance of fighting in an amphitheatre. As an option it must have seemed preferable to working as a slave in the hellish mines or on some of the *latifundiae*, the huge estates owned by senators where slaves were treated worse than dogs and life was brutal and short. Life as a gladiator, on the other hand, offered the possibility of fame and riches, leading finally – perhaps – to freedom.

The Ludus Magnus

An impressive three-storied building, the Ludus Magnus was started under Domitian and completed under Hadrian who reigned AD76–138. Built of brick-faced concrete like much of Rome, its courtyard had porticoes flanking its own arena, which measured 63 by 43m/69 by 47yd. The narrow *cavea* surrounding could seat about 3,000 spectators. The gladiators lived in rooms looking down on to the arena and seldom ventured out, except for the amphitheatre via a special tunnel.

▶ *Top right a view of the ruins shows how close the Ludus was to the Colosseum, while excavations bottom right show remains of the rooms that ran round the edges of its arena.*

▲ *A re-enactment in Merida's amphitheatre in Spain, of a fight between two gladiators, closely watched by an adjudicator.*

▼ *A typical pairing of a* murmillo*, a heavily armed gladiator (left) and a* retiarius*, a lightly armed fighter who danced nimbly to avoid his opponent's sword while trying to trap him in the net. A* lanista *(trainer) looks on from his horse. (Getty)*

The Ludus Matutinus

Literally meaning 'school of the morning', the Ludus Matutinus was for training *venatores,* the morning performers. It was situated near to the Ludus Magnus, to the south, and was about the same size. Here the animal fighters lived and learned their skills.

The Ludus Gallicus and Ludus Dacicus

Sited somewhere to the north of the Ludus Magnus, the Ludus Gallicus and Ludus Dacicus refer respectively to the Gauls and Dacians. Gaul (France) had long been a well-integrated province but wars against Dacia (modern Romania) reached a peak at this time. After Trajan's final conquest of Dacia in AD106, there was a flood of Dacian war captives to supply numerous recruits for the *ludi*. By then there were about 5,000 gladiators of all types living and training in the *ludi* in Rome.

LANISTAS

Discipline was extremely harsh – necessarily. Not only were some gladiators dangerous criminals but all had to learn very quickly the skills vital to survive in the arena. Each new gladiator had to swear to his *lanista* – his trainer, who was often also his owner; 'To obey the *lanista* in everything. To endure burning, imprisonment, flogging and even death by the sword'. This was an oath that was taken literally.

But, as the *lanista* had to make a substantial investment in purchasing and training a gladiator – whom he would then rent out to the editor actually paying for a show – he had every incentive to keep his gladiators alive as long as possible. Typically, if a gladiator were killed in the arena, the *editor* had to compensate the *lanista* by paying about 50 times the rental fee. The contract binding a gladiator to his *lanista* ran for an agreed length of time, often five or six years, after which the gladiator was free – assuming he lived that long. It has been calculated that gladiators had an 80–90% chance of surviving any one contest because *missio* (mercy) was granted to many of the defeated. By the time they reached the age of 30 most gladiators were too old to fight, but life expectancy in imperial Rome was not that much greater for poorer citizens.

A *lanista* would decide which type of gladiator best suited a new recruit. A heavy muscular man would be trained as a Thracian or *secutor,* while a lightly built man would become a *retiarius*. Specialist instructors called *doctores* taught each type of gladiator. Often *doctores* were retired gladiators, putting hard-earned skills to use.

Initial training

Basic training lasted up to six months. Swordsmen at first had to practise with extra-heavy weapons to build their muscles. The writer Vegetius around AD380 described the basic training then standard for both soldiers and gladiators: 'A stake was planted in the ground that the trainee treated as an opponent, now attacking his face, now threatening his sides, now trying to slash his knees and legs. He would draw back, leap forward

> Skill, discipline and art all combine to enable a gladiator to kill... Instruction makes it possible to kill and, once the slaying is done, there is glory.
>
> St Cyprian of Carthage, CAD250

and assault his imaginary opponent with all the energy and skill needed in a real fight. A novice had to be cautious to avoid exposing himself to wounds while trying to hit his enemy.' When these skills had been mastered, recruits fought with blunt weapons against other recruits, urged on or reprimanded by the *lanista*, who took a keen interest in his costly pupils.

Tiros

Once a novice had finished his training, he became a *tiro* (beginner). Before their first *munus*, tiros were ritually whipped to encourage them. For their first fight in the arena they were normally matched with other *tiros* – not out of kindness but because an experienced gladiator might kill them far too quickly, spoiling the fun. Sometimes, however, a *tiro* did face a veteran, as graffiti from Pompeii attest. A *tiro* called Attilius

▼ *A wounded gladiator in the amphitheatre at Pergamum being tended by Galen, the official doctor of the Ludus. Galen revolutionised the treatment of gladiators and reduced their mortality rate. Success in Pergamum led to him being called to Rome, where he became the emperor's physician. (Getty)*

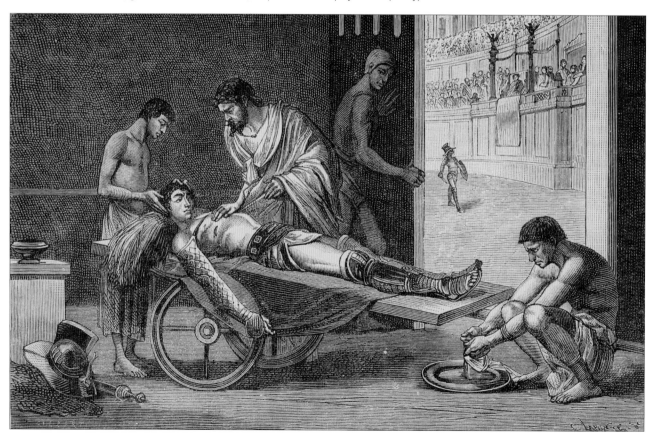

fought a *Thracian* called Hilarius with 14 victories to his name, and won! He went on to fight another veteran of 12 victories. Here too Attilius won – he must have been a superb fighter. When a *tiro* had won his first fight, he himself became a *veteranus,* veteran.

Veterans

How often gladiators fought each year depended on many factors, including the status of the fighter. A really successful gladiator would cost the *editor* – the man who paid for the event, whether he was a private individual or an emperor – much more than an unknown. Professor Mary Beard of Cambridge University thinks that in the 1st and 2nd centuries AD 'imperial gladiators' – those in the Colosseum – fought only about six to eight times a year, but it seems many gladiators wanted to fight more often. According to the philosopher Epictetus writing about AD120, 'among the imperial gladiators some get annoyed because no one leads them out to fight, or pairs them off in contests. They pray to the gods and ask the procurator to let them fight in the arena.'

HIERACHY IN THE LUDUS

The social organisation of a *ludus* partly resembled a prison. Many gladiators *were* effectively prisoners, some even being kept in chains in their cells. (A few volunteers could, however, come and go much as they pleased and even had women living with them.) Living conditions for the less fortunate could be very cramped, with two men sharing a cell only 2.5 by 1.5m/8 by 5ft. In the *ludus* at Pompeii, the ceilings of the gladiators' cells were so low they could never have stood up. Exercising in the *ludus* arena, or watching others rehearse from the *cavea* benches, must have been a welcome release for such inmates.

▼ *A re-enactor playing the part of a Roman surgeon at the Roman villa at Chedworth in Gloucestershire, England. Roman surgical instruments were generally very simple. (Alamy)*

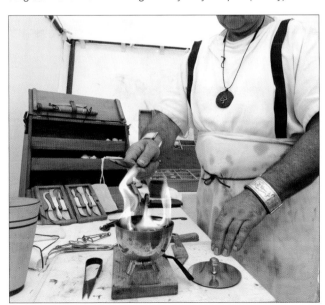

Every gladiator belonged to a particular *familia* or group but these were not always happy families. New recruits could face savage bullying from older fighters. Despite this, close friendships seem to have developed among gladiators, who would often help pay for a dead comrade's funeral.

Gladiators of each type were ranked into four grades, the top grade being the *primus palus* – literally, 'first stake' – echoing the rankings in the army. The great imperial *ludi* were commanded by a procurator of the equestrian (knightly) class, an experienced official appointed by the emperor who controlled the trainers, armourers, guards and medics.

HEALTH

The medical care gladiators of the Colosseum received was surprisingly good. *Unctores*, skilled masseurs, worked on twisted or strained muscles while *medici,* proper doctors, tended to more serious injuries. The greatest doctor of his age, Galen, made his name looking after gladiators. Gladiators also had a better or at least more abundant diet than many citizens, although they complained of its monotony.

Constant exercise, unusually attentive medical care and a better diet than most ordinary citizens combined to make most gladiators exceptionally fit. (It helped that they were generally young, few continuing in the arena beyond the age of 30.) Although the Latin motto *mens sana in corpore sano* means 'a healthy mind in a healthy body' and was a Roman ideal, many citizens were pretty unhealthy. Gladiators in contrast were generally fighting fit – until they were wounded or killed in the *munera*.

GALEN: THE GLADIATOR'S DOCTOR

Galen (AD129–204) was the greatest medical scientist of the Roman Empire. He was so highly reputed that his teachings were accepted, widely and uncritically, into the 19th century. Galen studied at Alexandria and then at Smyrna and Pergamum (both in western Turkey), before being appointed gladiatorial doctor to the *ludus* at Pergamum in AD157. There he revolutionised the care of gladiators.

His first concern was with their food. He thought that their diet of barley gruel mixed with beans made them flabby so he introduced more protein into their meals. He also became an expert at treating wounds, keeping gladiators alive far better than his predecessors had. In his four years at Pergamum only two gladiators died from wounds compared with the 60 who had died under his predecessor. His soaring prestige led to a summons to Rome in AD162, where he became personal physician to the emperors Marcus Aurelius, Commodus and Septimius Severus. Galen wrote prodigiously, synthesising the ancient world's medical, scientific and literary knowledge. He left some 350 works that shaped medical practice not only in Europe but also later across the Islamic world.

TYPES OF GLADIATOR

The word 'gladiator' comes from *gladius*, sword, which implies that most gladiators were skilled swordsmen, as were Rome's famous legionaries, but the suggestion is misleading. There were always many different types of gladiator and only some of them fought with swords. The rest relied mainly on other weapons such as tridents or spears.

▲ The 'typical' gladiator fought with some of the assorted arms and armour shown above. These are of course reconstructions.

▲ A legionary re-enactor in the typical full body armour of Roman soldier around the time the Colosseum was built. Note the long curved shields in the background with the legionary insignia on them. Gladiators' arms and armour in some ways mirrored and in other ways differed from those of soldiers. Most importantly, few gladiators wore much body armour.

▼ An re-enactor attempting to recreate the arms and very skimpy armour of a retiarius, a 'net man', the lightest-armed fighter in the arena. Note the lack of armour, the net in his right hand, and the pole of his trident, the head of which is not visible, in his left. Probably actual retiarii were slimmer and more lithe than this man.

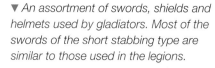

▼ An assortment of swords, shields and helmets used by gladiators. Most of the swords of the short stabbing type are similar to those used in the legions.

In the middle Republic (the 2nd century BC), when a *munus* was a simple affair with only a few paired-off fighters – all *damnati*, criminals condemned to be executed, or war captives – nearly all contestants used swords. A few may have had rudimentary lessons in duelling from soldiers. As the *munus* grew larger and more sophisticated, however, turning from funeral rite into elaborate entertainment-cum-electoral bribe, distinctive types of gladiator emerged. And gladiators became professionals.

Gladiators were divided into categories based on styles of armour, weapons and fighting. The categories were rather fluid and changed over time. Under the Republic five sorts of gladiators can be identified: *Samnite*, *Gaul*, *Thracian* (or *Thraex*), all of them heavily-armed swordsmen named after peoples that Rome had conquered, *eques* (horseman) and *provocator* (challenger). The first three types must have originated in war captives taken from those peoples, forced to fight each other to the death. By the time the Colosseum was completed, however, only the *Thracian* and *provocator* still survived as recognisable types. (As Samnites and Gauls had long been loyal allies of Rome by AD80, the names were changed possibly to avoid offending them – a rare example of Roman political correctness.)

By the middle of the first century AD five types of heavy swordsmen had emerged: the *Thracian*, *Secutor*, *Murmillo*, *Provocator* and *Hoplomachos*. They all wore distinctive helmets and armour. In the western half of the Empire at least, these types seem to have changed very little after AD100. While such swordsmen were the most prestigious and popular types of gladiator there were many other sorts, all adding to the variety of the arena.

THRACIAN

The *Thracian* originally came from Thrace, the southeastern corner of the Balkans now split between Greece, Turkey and Bulgaria. It was a wild, mountainous part of the world that took Rome a long time to subdue. Because of this there was a steady supply of war captives – of whom Spartacus was the most famous – after the wars against Mithridates, who ruled a Black Sea empire, in the 80s BC. Cicero, writing in 60BC, gives us the first mention of the *Thracian* gladiator, although Thrace only officially became a Roman province in AD48.

Unlike other sword-wielding gladiators with whom they could be paired, the *Thracian* carried a curved *sica* (a short curved sword) and a *parma* (a small rectangular curved shield). Weighing about 3kg/6.6lb the shield was notably lighter than the ones carried by similar gladiators. He also had a *manica* (a leather sleeve on his exposed right arm), *fasciae* (bands of protective leather around his legs and thighs) and two metal greaves (leg guards). The most imposing part of his armour was his helmet. This had a flamboyant high crest topped either by a plume or by a bronze griffin, a mythological beast compounded of a lion and eagle. The *Thracian* thus combined some of the agility of a lightly armed fighter with the protection enjoyed by other swordsmen. This combination perhaps accounts for his long popularity.

Supporters of the *Thracian*, who included the emperor Caligula, were called *parmularii*, after the small shield a *Thracian* carried. Caligula even fought duels as a *Thracian*, though not in a public arena, and placed some of them in command of his German bodyguard. The emperor Titus later also publicly supported the *Thraeces*, joining in the abuse that the crowds yelled at their rivals. The *Thracian* was often pitted against the *Murmillo* and the *hoplomachus*. The torso of all these gladiators was bare, unlike that of an actual soldier.

MURMILLO

One of the most heavily armed of all gladiators, the *murmillo* (sometimes spelt myrmillo) probably evolved from the earlier Gaul gladiator. He was most notable for his helmet, which had a very prominent angular crest. His name possibly comes from the Greek word *mormulos*, a kind of fish, because the helmets of at least some *murmillones* had fish on them. He was also called *murmillo* because his typical opponent in the arena was the *retiarius*, who with his trident and nets was often nicknamed 'the fisherman'. At times the *murmillo* also

▼ *Kirk Douglas (left) stars as Spartacus in Stanley Kubrik's 1960 film. A Thracian gladiator, Spartacus was one of the rebel slave leaders in Rome's Third Servile War. (Alamy)*

fought the *Thracian* and when he did he almost always won, at least according to Martial.

The *murmillo* had a very large shield, oblong and concave in form, that protected most of his body. He also had greaves on his right arm and his left leg – the most vulnerable of the respective limbs, the gladiator's shield covering the left arm and his sword his right leg. His weapon was the usual short straight Roman stabbing sword.

Like the *Thracian*, the *murmillo* often attracted tribes of keen fans who were called *scutarii* after his *scutum* or shield. Nero was a keen *scutarius*, showering Spiculus, his favourite *murmillo,* with lavish gifts. Later, when Nero had lost his throne and was about to lose his life, he begged Spiculus to kill him – in vain. The deposed emperor had to take his own life. The despotic Domitian became a fanatical *scutarius*, regarding any criticism of them as a personal insult – indeed tantamount to blasphemy, because he increasingly regarded himself as divine. He had some *parmularii* (as followers of the *Thracians* were known), whom he found particularly annoying, burnt alive in the arena.

SECUTORES

Secutor in Latin means 'pursuer' and pursuit was what a *secutor* did. Matched normally with a *retiarius*, which was the most popular of all pairing of gladiators throughout the empire, he would pursue the agile and evasive net man around the arena, trying to close in and trap him for a kill. The *secutor's* other name was *contraretiarius*, meaning anti-*retiarius*. A *secutor* had a semi-cylindrical shield and was armed like a legionary with a short stabbing sword but only had a padded, segmented arm-guard and a short greave, like most gladiators. The *secutor's* most distinctive feature was his smooth helmet, which had no crest, brim or visor but only two tiny holes for the eyes. The lack of decorations on the helmet gave the *retiarius* less scope to entangle him with the net while the small eye holes protected a *secutor* from the prongs of his adversary's trident. But such a helmet also restricted his field of vision, so ensuring that their fights were lengthened. The almost blank helmet gave him a threatening, inhuman appearance in the arena, adding to the dramatic contrast with the lightly armed, vulnerable-looking *retiarius*.

PROVOCATORES

The *provacotor* or 'challenger' originated in the late Republic but continued long into the imperial era. Another type of gladiator mentioned by Cicero, he had a helmet with a visor and a neck guard at the back but it was unbrimmed. Like all gladiators except the *eques* he wore a *subligaculum* (an undergarment often in the form of a loincloth) and had a greave on his left leg and segmented lower arm-guards. A *provacotor's* shield was rectangular and semi-cylindrical. His most distinctive aspect was his breastplate, which was strapped to his body. The *provocator* was the only type of gladiator who wore any protective armour on his torso. This gave him a theoretical defensive advantage in combat but also made him heavier and slower-moving. *Provacotores* were unusual among the 'heavy' gladiators in that they were

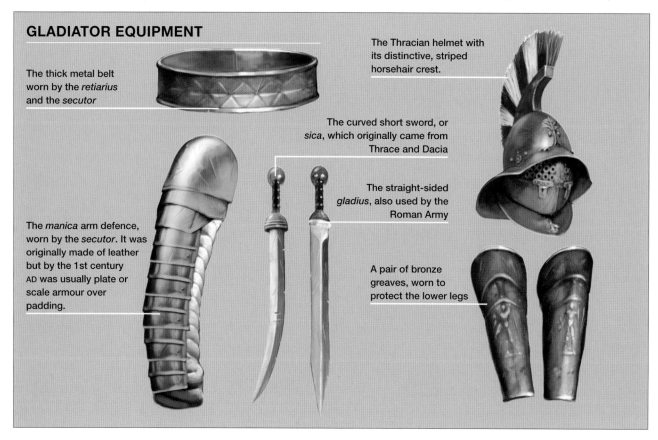

GLADIATOR EQUIPMENT

The thick metal belt worn by the *retiarius* and the *secutor*

The *manica* arm defence, worn by the *secutor*. It was originally made of leather but by the 1st century AD was usually plate or scale armour over padding.

The Thracian helmet with its distinctive, striped horsehair crest.

The curved short sword, or *sica*, which originally came from Thrace and Dacia

The straight-sided *gladius*, also used by the Roman Army

A pair of bronze greaves, worn to protect the lower legs

seldom matched against other types of fighter but mostly fought each other. In their armour and style of fighting they came closest to contemporary legionaries.

HOPLOMACHUS

The word *hoplomachus* means literally 'fighter with shield' in Greek. This gladiator type was derived from the *hoplite*, the standard Greek or Macedonian heavy infantrymen who had fought so successfully against the armies of Persia and later, with far less success, against those of Rome. Like the *Thracian*, the *hoplomachus* had a *manica* (leather sleeve) on his exposed right arm, long quilted linen leggings, and carried a *parma*, a small circular and concave shield. He fought usually with a straight sword and sometimes with a thrusting spear, as Greek hoplites had done. He was often paired with a *murmillo* or *Thracian,* couplings that provided variety for spectators but also encouraged prolonged duelling between two well-matched swordsmen. All these gladiators wore a *subligaculum* but no other clothes.

RETIARIUS

Easy to identify, the *retiarius* or net man – his name derives from his *rete* (net) that he carried – differed from the other gladiators, all of whom in some ways still resembled soldiers, in being almost unarmoured. Perhaps because of this, he was the lowest ranking of all the main gladiator types. Wearing no helmet and almost no armour and carrying no shield, his principal weapon was a *fuscina* (trident) not a sword or spear. He also carried an auxiliary weapon, a dagger. On his left arm he wore a *manica* and on his left shoulder a *galerus*, a long steel shoulder-guard that no other gladiator wore. He needed his *galerus* because he was extremely vulnerable to attacks on his left side. The *galerus*, often decorated with a crab, dolphin, anchor or other nautical motif, gave his throat and lower face some protection but otherwise he was totally exposed to slashing swords, being bareheaded and bare-legged as well as bare-chested. He made up for this by being exceptionally agile, able to dance around his heavily armoured opponent until the latter grew exhausted and stumbled. A *retiarius* would then try to throw his lead-weighted net over the swordsman, usually a *murmillo* or *secutor*, and so entrap him. He could use his trident to wound his opponent, if necessary finishing the heavier man off close up with his dagger. But the odds generally favoured the *secutor* or *murmillo.* No remains of a *retiarius's* net have yet been found but the evidence from numerous mosaics is revealing.

EQUITES

Markedly different from other fighters were the *equites*, horsemen. They had the honour of presenting the first combat of the afternoon following the initial *pompa*. After galloping resplendent in plumed helmets with visors on white horses around the arena, they then charged briefly with lances before dismounting to fight on foot. This might seem an anti-climax but full-scale medieval-style jousting

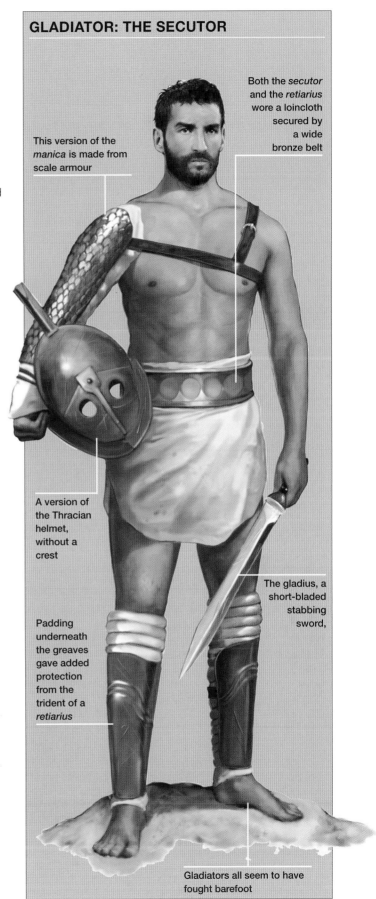

GLADIATOR: THE SECUTOR

This version of the *manica* is made from scale armour

Both the *secutor* and the *retiarius* wore a loincloth secured by a wide bronze belt

A version of the Thracian helmet, without a crest

The gladius, a short-bladed stabbing sword,

Padding underneath the greaves gave added protection from the trident of a *retiarius*

Gladiators all seem to have fought barefoot

GLADIATOR: MURMILLO

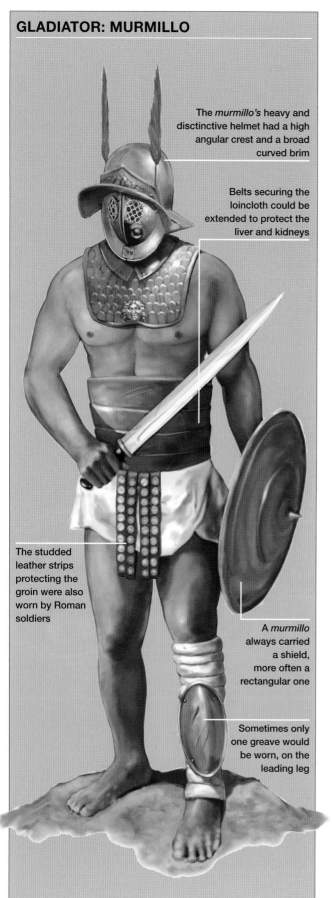

The *murmillo's* heavy and disctinctive helmet had a high angular crest and a broad curved brim

Belts securing the loincloth could be extended to protect the liver and kidneys

The studded leather strips protecting the groin were also worn by Roman soldiers

A *murmillo* always carried a shield, more often a rectangular one

Sometimes only one greave would be worn, on the leading leg

was almost impossible for ancient horsemen. The Romans lacked stirrups, very important to keep a rider in the saddle after hitting – or being hit by – an opponent with a lance. This is one reason why cavalry long played only a minor part in Roman warfare. They also usually played only a minor and preliminary role in the *munera*. In contrast to other gladiators who wore only a loincloth, *equites* wore short tunics like real soldiers.

ESSEDARII

Although the Colosseum was too small for proper chariot races – these were held in the much larger Circus Maximus – chariots driven by gladiators called *essedarii* for a time delighted the novelty-mad Romans in the arena. *Essedarii* derives from *essedarum*, a light chariot used in Celtic Britain – Queen Boudicca of the Iceni would have ridden one. Although their first appearance in the arena may date from Julius Caesar's abortive invasions of 55 and 54BC, they only became a regular feature in the Roman arena following Claudius's conquest of Britain in AD43. As in real battles, the *essedarius* seems to have dismounted for the main phase of the fighting. The skills required to manage a chariot with two horses were not widely taught in the *ludus*, however, so this type of gladiator seems to have vanished once a ready supply of British captives dried up after AD100.

VENATORES

For a long time *venatores* (hunters) were considered distinct from other gladiators and the main games. *Venationes* were often staged in different places while *venatores* themselves were often recruited from local people in Africa and Asia who knew how to hunt animals in their own part of the wild. By AD80 the *venationes* had become an essential part of the day's entertainment, and a special school for such hunters, the Ludus Matutinus, the morning school – so called because the mornings were the normal time for *venationes* – was established later near the Colosseum. Nonetheless, *Venatores* were seen as being different from normal gladiators. Like the *retiarii* they wore no armour but they had a long, effective spear with which to fight the animals they faced in the ring. They also wore tunics, not just loincloths. They never had the same prestige as the heavy gladiators but they appealed to the games-mad emperor Commodus, who killed thousands of animals.

Do I need to tell you of the purple wraps and oils used by women? ... What modesty can you expect in a woman who chooses to wear a helmet, abjures her own sex and delights in feats of arms? Yet she would not really choose to be a man, for she knows the superior joys of womanhood… Yet these are women who find the finest of robes too heavy for them, whose delicate skin is irritated by the purest silks. See how she pants!

Juvenal, *Satire VI*, CAD100

▶ *In this mosaic from around 200AD in Spain the* retiarius, *who is clearly named as Kalendo, and his opponent the* secutor *Astynax are shown at differing stages of the combat. In the topmost Astynax appears to be about to triumph, despite being entangled in the net, for Kalendo has fallen to the ground. In the lower part of the mosaic the same two fighters have reversed roles and Kalendo seemingly now has the upper hand. Behind each stand their respective* lanistae *or trainers, advising the gladiators and urging them on. (Alamy)*

FEMALE GLADIATORS

Women gladiators in the arena were always something of a rarity, even an oddity. A few scholars such as Professor Beard have queried their existence, but archaeological and literary sources alike generally confirm that, at least occasionally, women fought in the Colosseum and in other arenas. A bas-relief from the Greek city of Halicarnassus (now Bodrum, Turkey) shows two female gladiators, who resemble *Thraeces* with swords and shields but without helmets, fighting each other. They are named underneath as Amazonia and Achillia, suitable stage names. As Roman society was deeply sexist and women were regarded as the weaker and inferior sex, female gladiators excited scorn and mockery rather than admiration.

The first female gladiators appeared in the very lax period of the late Republic as a positive mania for gladiators grew. Augustus issued decrees trying to control them but with little success. Finally in AD19 a *Senatus Consultum* (decree of the Senate) forbade women of the two upper classes, the

▼ *Two well-armed female gladiators, Amazonia and Achillia fight in a carving from Halicarnassus. Women gladiators were a rarity in the arena but certainly existed. (Alamy)*

senators and knights, from appearing on stage or in the arena to preserve their aristocratic dignity.

The inventive Nero in AD66 organised a *munus* for Tiridates, the visiting king of Armenia, where all the performers were 'Ethiopian' (meaning in fact from the Sudan) women, dwarfs and children – a deliberately ridiculous combination. On a couple of occasions Nero also forced Roman noblewomen, along with noblemen, to perform in public, in the circus, on stage and in the arena, but with blunted weapons. He was severely criticised for breaching aristocratic dignity by doing this, but he also favoured other non-lethal contests such as athletics and dancing, part of his overall philhellenism (love of all things Greek). Petronius, one of Nero's courtiers until he fell from favour, mentions in his novel *Satyricon an essedaria*, a female charioteer from Britain.

Later, Domitian held a nocturnal *munus* by torchlight where women gladiators fought each other, an event warmly praised by the sycophantic Martial. In AD200, the emperor Septimius Severus banned women gladiators altogether, citing the fact the 'women in this contest fought so energetically and savagely they made other aristocratic women the subject of jokes'. His motives were therefore social, not humanitarian.

DEMIGODS AND HEROES: GLADIATORS' NAMES

Many gladiators came from distant corners of the empire, or even from beyond its frontiers. When they reached Rome, they might have had names that Romans found barbarously uncouth and ridiculous. So, like modern film stars, most fighters changed their names to ones that Roman audiences could recognise. These usually suggested courage, glamour and skill – the essential attributes of any gladiator. As the Romans knew their ancient myths well, gladiators often took the name of a hero or demigod. Hercules, Alexander, Ajax, Diomedes, Spartacus (Spartan) and Perseus were all common gladiator names. Others, wanting to stress their brutal strength, chose Ferox (ferocious), Pugnax (combative), Triumphus (triumph), Tigris (tiger), Leo (lion) or Invictus (unconquered). A lightly armed *retiarius* might choose a name like Rapidus (quick) or Callidromus (speedy) while handsome fighters wanting to impress female – or male – spectators with their looks as much as their skills chose effeminate names such as Narcissus, after the boy who fell in love with his own beauty, Eros or Amethyst. A famously handsome gladiator, who called himself Hermes, after the Greek messenger-god, was dubbed by Martial the 'focus of groupies' affections. Other gladiators chose names emphasising old-fashioned virtues such as Verus (truthful) and Priscus (traditional).

SPARTACUS

The most famous gladiator of all is Spartacus. Leader of the greatest slave revolt in antiquity, which for a moment threatened Rome's very existence, his rebellion against a servile fate made him a legend in his lifetime and ever since. In the 20th century he inspired people as disparate as the German revolutionaries of 1919 – the Spartacists, led by Rosa Luxemburg – and Hollywood stars such as Kirk Douglas in the eponymous film of 1960, as well as the ballet *Spartacus* by the Soviet composer Khachaturian in 1956.

Despite his name, Spartacus did not come from Sparta but from Thrace, then outside the empire. Little is known of his early life but he may have served for a time in the Roman army, for he clearly understood military tactics. Details of his life are found in the works of two writers of the 2nd century AD, Plutarch and Appian, although they can contradict each other. Spartacus became a deserter, was captured and sold to Lentulus Batiatus, a *lanista* who ran a *ludus* in Capua in 73BC.

Spartacus, already renowned for his strength, soon showed leadership qualities. With 70 fellow prisoners he seized knives from the kitchen and broke out of the *ludus*. They found a wagon full of gladiator weapons with which they routed the first soldiers they met outside the city. Significantly, they took these troops' weapons, throwing away the arena arms they considered dishonourable or useless. They then chose Spartacus as their leader, with two Gauls, Crixus and Oenomaus, as his lieutenants.

Spartacus led his band up Mt Vesuvius (dormant at the time). There a Roman force led by Claudius Glaber besieged them, meaning to starve them out. 'There was only one way up the hill,' wrote Plutarch, 'and that was a narrow, difficult one, closely guarded by Glaber. Every other route led only to steep precipitous cliffs. The summit, however, was covered in wild vines. From these the gladiators cut off all the branches they needed, twisting them into long ladders that reached down from the top of the cliff to the plain below… The Romans knew nothing of all this, so the gladiators managed to get round behind and surprise the Romans with an unexpected attack, routing them and capturing their camp. Soon they were joined by many herdsmen and shepherds, all reputedly "strong, agile men". Some were armed as regular infantry and others as scouts and light troops.'

Rome, preoccupied with wars in Spain and the East, at first did not take the revolt seriously. When another army was defeated near Herculaneum, escapee slaves in tens of thousands flocked to join Spartacus, swelling his ranks to 70,000. With the horses they captured they formed a cavalry wing and roamed through Italy plundering, despite Spartacus's efforts to restrain them. Realising there was no real chance of final success against Rome's huge

manpower, Spartacus tried to strike north to escape across the Alps. However Crixus, who wanted to carry on plundering Italy, took some Spanish and German gladiators with him, soon being killed in southern Italy.

Meanwhile Spartacus, after defeating two separate consular armies in northern Italy, turned the tables on the Romans by forcing 300 captured legionaries to fight each other to amuse his own troops. He now apparently thought of attacking Rome itself and moved south again, but Rome had awoken to its peril. Crassus, an experienced general commanding six legions – about 30,000 men – was sent in pursuit and managed to trap the gladiator army in the toe of Italy, building a wall across the peninsula. On the third attempt Spartacus broke through this barrier but his numbers were much depleted.

Finally, after killing two centurions in hand-to-hand fighting, Spartacus himself was killed in 70BC. His body was never found but 6,000 of his followers were crucified along the road

▲ *Kirk Douglas in the role of Spartacus in the 1960 film of that name. Spartacus led the greatest slave revolt in Roman history in 73BC. A Thracian by origin despite his name, he defied all Rome's armies for three years before being overwhelmed by Rome's immense military power. (Alamy)*

from Capua to Rome in a terrible warning to anyone thinking of future revolts. Over a distance of nearly 200km/125 miles, this meant a cross every 30m/33yds. This grisly retribution worked; there were no further large-scale gladiator or slave revolts in Italy. Wisely, the Romans broke up the huge gladiator schools at Capua into smaller units, realising the dangers they posed. Whether Spartacus ever really dreamt of abolishing slavery, as some recent admirers have suggested, remains unknown. There is no evidence to suggest that he was influenced by Greek philosophical ideals of human brotherhood, as a few Romans were, but his name remains an inspiration.

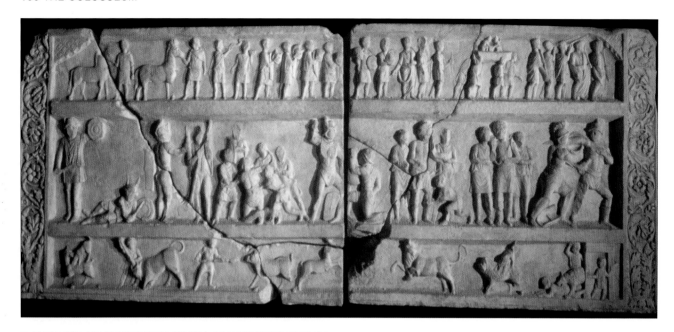

PRISCUS AND VERUS

Far more typical of Roman gladiators were two
outstanding fighters of the reign of Titus (AD79–81), Priscus
and Verus. Like many experienced gladiators, these two
veterans of the arena had fought and survived many
contests. They were certainly heavily armed gladiators,
possibly *murmillones or Thraeces,* and their duel probably
took place as part of the grand inauguration of the
Colosseum in AD80. It is the only gladiatorial combat for
which we have a full written record.

After an exhaustive but inconclusive fight, with first
one and then the other seeming to gain the upper hand,
Verus and Priscus had effectively arrived at a stalemate,
something almost without precedent in the arena. Their
equal fortitude and skills so impressed spectators that
they demanded *missio* for both, something Titus was
reluctant to grant. But, finally surrendering to the vocal
demands of the crowd, Titus granted to them both the
palm of liberty, the crown of victory and a large cash
sum, a rare happy ending in the Colosseum.

> Priscus and Verus, while with Equal Might,
> Prolong'd an obstinate and doubtful fight.
> The People oft their mission [release] did desire,
> But Caesar from the law would not retire,
> Which did the Prize and Victory Unite,
> Yet gave them what Encouragement he might…
> In the end, howe'er, the Strife was equal found,
> Both fought alike and both alike gave ground.
> So that the Palm was upon each conferred,
> Their undecided Valour this deserved.
> Under no Prince before we e'er did see
> That two should fight and both should Victors be.
> Martial, *Liber de Spectaculis,* trans. Thomas Killigrew

▲ *A marble relief from Pompeii of c50–20BC depicting
gladiatorial games. The whole sculpture, which is made of
several fragments, was originally carved on the side of a tomb
at the Maritime Necropolis in Pompeii. This is very appropriate
as* munera, *gladiatorial games, originated in games given in
honour of the dead. (Getty)*

AUCTORATI: THE VOLUNTEERS

Not every gladiator was a slave or war captive. Some free
men – and even a few free women – were volunteers, called
auctorati, who sold their freedom to a *lanista* for a certain
time for a lump sum. As the Roman historian Livy (59BC–AD17)
wrote, 'they put their blood up for sale'. *Auctorati* accepted
the same gruelling regime and dangers as any other gladiator.
The usual reason to volunteer for this hard, dangerous life
was destitution. For the financially desperate, life in the arena
could offer a last hope of restoring their fortunes. The poet
Horace (65–8BC), talking of a bankrupt, said he had only
three options left: to become a gardener, carriage driver or
gladiator. The last was the most perilous choice but it was
also the most glamorous, offering the outside chance of
gaining a large sum and retiring early.

The glamour of the arena at the peak of 'gladiator mania',
stretching from around the years 50BC to about AD40,
attracted wealthier men too, including some nobles, despite
the fact that gladiators were ranked as *infami*. The historian
Samuel Dill (1844–1924) suggested several reasons why
richer men enlisted: 'The splendour of arms, the ostentatious
pomp of the scene of combat, the applause of thousands
of spectators on the crowded benches and the fascination
of danger.' But everyone who became a real gladiator – as
opposed to just fighting the odd bout in the arena – lost all
rights as a citizen. Roman citizenship conferred substantial
benefits, including exemption from corporal punishment and
crucifixion. Over the centuries, however, these volunteers
constituted only a small minority of fighters in the arena.

GLADIATORS AS SOLDIERS

As both gladiators and soldiers were highly trained fighters, gladiators might be recruited into the army during crises. Their record as soldiers, however, was distinctly patchy. Mark Anthony, the great rival of Octavius (later Augustus), raised a force of some 3,000 gladiators in Asia Minor for his final conflict in 31BC but Actium, the deciding battle of that civil war, was fought before they could see action. Far from abandoning Anthony, however, the gladiators fought on until lack of supplies forced them to disband.

Later Gaius Caligula, one of the maddest of all emperors, recruited gladiators for his bodyguard, but they did not save him from assassination. In the civil wars of AD68 and 69, two of the rivals for the imperial throne, Otho and Vitellius, mobilised gladiators, but these arena-trained fighters proved of little use against skilled soldiers. Gladiators were trained for individual close combat, not for fighting in ranks. This inadequacy did not prevent Marcus Aurelius, during the great crisis of his reign in AD166–167 when German invasions threatened Italy, from recruiting gladiators. They were badly needed to replace soldiers killed by the plague. These new troops were called, perhaps euphemistically, *obsequentes* ('obedient'). His move proved unpopular with the Roman people, who suspected their philosophy-loving emperor of trying to curtail the games and interest them in philosophy instead.

The process could go the other way. In AD195, when the new emperor Septimius Severus sacked all the elite Praetorian Guard, replacing them with his own more loyal troops, some ex-Praetorians voluntarily enrolled as gladiators.

> For gladiators and soldiers alike, it is keen and quick intelligence coupled with sharpness and resourcefulness that protects men against defeat.   Cicero

▼ *In this 3rd-century mosaic the top scene shows two* murmillo *gladiators, the crossed out 'O' after the name Maternus shows he has lost. In the lower scene two* equites, *identifiable by their sleeveless tunics, fight on foot. (Alamy)*

THE GLADIATOR EMPEROR

Such was the glamour of the games that even some emperors played at being gladiators. Both Caligula (AD37–41) and Nero (AD54–68) 'fought' against opponents who took care to lose, gracefully accepting the odd loss of a nose or an ear to please their emperor; one who did not, when facing Caligula, lost his life for his impudence. But these early emperors did not fight in public, aware that to do so might harm their imperial image. By the time Commodus succeeded his father Marcus Aurelius in AD180, however, such considerations seem to have mattered less.

Commodus, who from the start totally neglected affairs of state, was at first a mild-mannered ruler, but a botched assassination attempt in AD182 tipped him into paranoia. He handed power over to a series of favourites and retreated to his villa outside Rome. There he amused himself with his huge harem – reputedly it had 300 concubines and 300 catamites – and with practising his gladiatorial skills in his private arena. He claimed to have taken part in 1,000 contests. (Whether or not Commodus really *was* the son of the high-minded Marcus Aurelius has long been debated. There were rumours that the empress Faustina had had an affair with a gladiator and Commodus was the unenviable result. But in his portrait busts Commodus does look much like the previous emperor.)

After several favourites had been executed to appease the mob, Commodus decided to return to the capital and display his now unsurpassed powers as a gladiator – in the Colosseum itself. A fire that ravaged the city revealed his now-rampant megalomania, for he decided to rename the city Commodiana after himself. Similarly, the months of the year were relabelled after his 12 names, as were the legions. To celebrate the dawning Era of Commodus, he threw elaborate games at the very end of AD192. The chief performer was of course Commodus, imperial superstar.

▼ *Joaquin Phoenix as the depraved emperor Commodus (AD180–192) in the film* Gladiator *(2000). No other emperor matched Commodus's passion for the games. He actually fought in the arena himself, something unprecedented and unrepeated in Roman history. (Alamy)*

Commodus had taken to impersonating Hercules, the muscular Greek hero and demigod, carrying a club and wearing a lion skin. But for these great games he wore a robe of purple with gold spangled stars and a gold crown. He did not march into the arena like a normal contestant but strutted out on a special catwalk high above the sand, where he was safe from the animals.

He started off by killing 100 bears trapped in nets with spears or arrows – he was certainly a good shot – before proceeding to slaughter ostriches by the score. Then, clutching a bird's bloodied head, he approached the seats where the senators sat and thrust it towards them, as if threatening them with a similar fate. The senator and historian Cassius Dio, who like other senators had to attend the games to keep his life, claimed that he only managed to stop himself laughing aloud at the ludicrous sight by frantically chewing laurel leaves. By then the emperor and Senate had become the most bitter of enemies, although Commodus's largesse ensured that the people still loved him. Soon afterwards he was assassinated by his attendants. He is summed up superbly by Edward Gibbon:

He (Commodus) was the first of the Roman emperors totally devoid of taste for the pleasures of understanding. Nero himself excelled, or affected to excel, in the elegant arts of music and poetry… But Commodus from his earliest infancy discovered an aversion to whatever was rational or liberal and a fond attachment to the amusements of the populace: the sports of the circus and the amphitheatre, the combats of gladiators and the hunting of wild beasts…

On the appointed day the various motives of flattery, fear and curiosity attracted to the amphitheatre an innumerable multitude of spectators; and some degree of applause was deservedly bestowed on the uncommon skill of the imperial performer. Whether he aimed at the head or heart of the animal, the wound was alike certain and mortal. With arrows, whose point was shaped into the form of a crescent, Commodus often intercepted the rapid career and cut aside the long bony neck of the ostrich. A panther was let loose and the archer waited until he had leaped upon a trembling malefactor [condemned criminal]. In the same instant the shaft flew, the beast dropt dead and the man remained unhurt. The dens of the amphitheatre disgorged at once a hundred lions; a hundred darts from the unerring hand of Commodus laid them dead as they ran raging round the arena. Neither the huge bulk of the elephant nor the scaly hide of the rhinoceros could defend them from his stroke… In all these exhibitions the securest precautions were used to protect the person of the Roman Hercules (Commodus) from the desperate spring of any savage…

But the meanest of the populace was affected with shame and indignation when they beheld their sovereign enter the lists as a gladiator, and glory in a profession which the laws and manners of the Romans had branded with the justest note of infamy. He chose the habit and arms of the Secutor, whose combat with the Retiarius formed one of the most lively scenes in the bloody sport of the amphitheatre. The Secutor was armed with an helmet, sword and buckler; his naked antagonist had only a large net and trident; with the one he endeavoured to entangle, with the other to dispatch his enemy. If he missed the first throw he was obliged to fly from the pursuit of the Secutor, till he had prepared his net for a second cast. The emperor fought in this character 735 several times. These glorious achievements were carefully recorded in the public acts of the empire; and that he might omit no circumstance of infamy, he received from the common fund of gladiators a stipend so exorbitant that it became a new and most ignominious tax upon the Roman people.

Edward Gibbon, *History of the Decline and Fall of the Roman Empire* Book I, 1776

▼ *Commodus associated himself with the Greek hero Hercules, and near the end of his reign commissioned this bust of himself dressed as the hero, which still survives.*

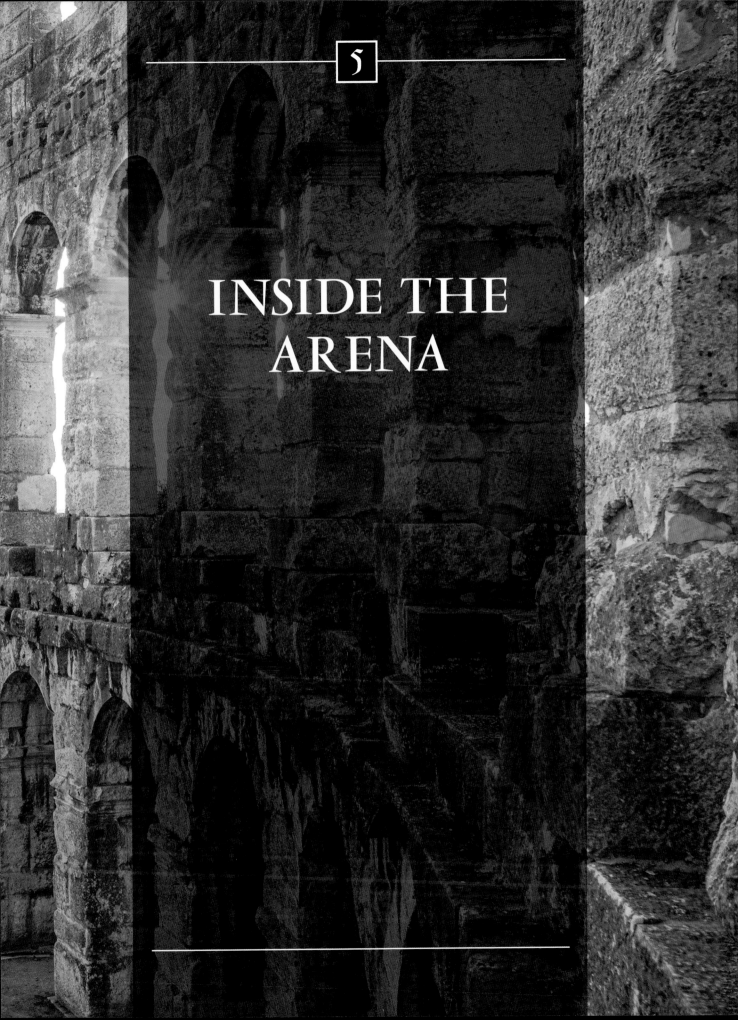

5

INSIDE THE ARENA

THE SPECTATORS

From the day of its inauguration, the Colosseum was ranked among Rome's greatest attractions. Only the Circus Maximus rivalled its instant appeal to visitors and to residents of the world's capital. Tickets – for a whole day or a series of days – gave admittance to entertainments in which the emperor tried to dazzle the people with novel or unprecedentedly lavish shows.

The Colosseum did not hold games on a regular basis, instead they were held intermittently, like a football match or similar sporting event today. Nor were the *munera* continuous. When ancient writers spoke of the 123 days of games given by the emperor Trajan to celebrate his conquest of Dacia (Romania) in AD106 that involved 10,000 gladiators and the slaughter of 11,000 wild animals, they did not mean 123 consecutive days of events. Such an orgy would have exhausted the imperial treasury, gladiator schools and audiences alike. But as the calendar filled up with more and more public holidays – granted by emperors keen to please the fickle populace – the Flavian Amphitheatre must have become much the busiest arena in the whole empire.

The audience at the Colosseum was not a cross-section of Roman society. Instead of being composed of howling mobs of poor Romans desperate for cheap thrills – as Hollywood, has often depicted it – it was actually composed mostly of richer Romans. The upper and middle classes were disproportionately represented, taking about 60% of the seats although they made up a far smaller proportion of the population. This was a deliberate policy, one that both mirrored and emphasised the stratification of Rome's very unequal society. It was also probably inevitable, due to limitations of space.

The maximum capacity of the Colosseum was 50,000–55,000, according to current estimates. By AD80 the population of Rome had passed the 1 million mark and it continued to grow for decades. Adult male citizens – a category that may have included boys over the age of 16 – made up at least 200,000 of this number, the rest of the inhabitants being women, children, non-citizens and the numerous slaves. So, entrance to the city's one amphitheatre had to be rationed.

▼ *Crowds filling the* cavea *at the amphitheatre in Verona. But now they come to see opera not gladiatorial games.*

TICKETS FOR FREE

Tesserae (tickets) for events in the Colosseum, as for other games and the public baths, were probably always free, being one of the perks of Roman citizenship. This did not mean that they were always freely available. While the elite could always rely on a good seat being kept for them, how most tickets were distributed remains unknown. We know that some were reserved in block bookings for the *collegia,* the guilds to which many Roman men belonged, or for particular groups such as the rich citizens of Cádiz, in Spain. (This particular arrangement lasted for centuries.) Powerful men also distributed them as gifts to their dependents – status in Rome was partly based on how many such 'clients' a wealthy man could command.

Other tickets seemed to have been given effectively at random. As in much of Roman life, there was a strong element of luck for poorer citizens in getting hold of tickets. Rich senators and knights were, however, always assured of prime seats. No actual tickets to the Colosseum survive but examples from amphitheatres elsewhere – small tokens of wood or lead – give details of the specified seat or block of seats.

▼ *In the well-preserved theatre at Jerash, Jordan, re-enactors today drive Roman-style chariots.*

▲ *A male and female Roman citizen in formal dress, typical of the higher-ranking members of the Colosseum's audience.*

▲ *The remains of the Circus Maximus, Rome's largest public arena, which hosted chariot races and other events.*

The Circus Maximus by contrast, which hosted grand chariot races as well as gladiatorial games and wild beast hunts, could seat up to 300,000. So the Circus far more than the Colosseum was where the Roman people en masse revealed its true tastes and feelings. Support for rival chariot teams in the Circus could lead to riots but in the much more tightly controlled Colosseum no riots seem to have occurred at all. Further, the arena's nearly circular shape was well suited to staging *munera*. Its ellipse allowed the whole audience to see the full spectacle, which the *spina* (central barrier) of the long Circus Maximus could prevent. It also allowed upper-class spectators to be clearly seen, something very important in Rome's status-conscious society. In the Colosseum the audience was always a part of the show – yet another reason that there was a premium on seats in Rome's one amphitheatre.

▼ *Model of the Colosseum, cut away to show the* cavea, *part of the* hypogeum *and the tunnel to the Ludus Magnus. (Getty)*

CROWD CONTROL ROMAN STYLE

Getting 50,000 or more excited spectators smoothly to and from their intended seats in the amphitheatre presented a logistical challenge that the Romans rose to with customary skill. For the Colosseum the architects devised highly effective methods of controlling spectators tightly while ensuring efficient circulation of the crowds surging in and out. The aim was to get people swiftly to their correct place while segregating the different classes – and sexes – carefully so that grand senators, for example, never needed to rub shoulders with plain proletarians.

The wide travertine-paved circular piazza around the amphitheatre was divided into sections by iron cables attached to a row of 80 stone posts encircling the building. Only five of these posts survive, now leaning in at a drunken angle. Crowds of eager Romans who had been milling around from first light – the Roman world ran mostly according to the sun, artificial lighting being expensive and scanty -– were marshalled into groups before entry. The piazza gave easy access to every part of the amphitheatre's facade, which had 80 bays or entrances, 76 of them numbered. The other four on each axis were reserved for the emperor and for the performers. Each bay opened on to a radial passageway converging towards the centre of the arena.

From these passageways a complex series of circular galleries called *ambulacra* allowed arriving spectators to move along laterally beneath the *cavea*. Each of the *ambulacra* led directly into the internal vaulted spaces beneath the tiers of seats. Radial passageways led either to the staircases between the different levels or to the arched entrances to the *cavea*. Nicknamed *vomitoria* – because they vomited forth crowds of people – these arches gave direct access to the tiers of seating, or conversely led in to further galleries deep within the amphitheatre. These galleries very seldom led to dead ends, however, although they now often appear to do so thanks to botched restorations. Some modern engineers estimate that in an emergency the whole audience, 50,000

▲ *The piazza encircling the Colosseum where crowds would gather before performances, be marshalled into groups, then surge into the amphitheatre to find their seats.*

strong, could have been evacuated in just 12 minutes, not something every modern stadium could do. The *vomitoria* were therefore well named.

Ordinary spectators *ie* not senators, knights or Vestal Virgins, entered by one of the 76 numbered arches and then climbed up the steep stairways of the outer galleries, which were plastered and painted, until they reached their designated *vomitorium* (arched opening). To protect people as they passed the 3m/10ft drop from the seats into the stairwells there were stone or marble balustrades in place. These were carved with plants or animals such as hunting dogs, dolphins and mythological beasts such as griffins. Accidents still happened, however, in the mad rush for seats.

▼ *Three of the 80 crowd control bollards that went round the amphitheatre, with heavy cables strung in between. (Getty)*

▲ *Even in ruins the almost vertiginous rise of the* cavea *demonstrates that height inside the Colosseum was in inverse relation to status; the lower your seating, the higher your rank.*

Seating conditions for ordinary people were very cramped. Lines cut into the stone seats in other amphitheatres – the original seats from the Colosseum have not survived, although some have been reconstructed – show that the average space allocated to spectators was only 40cm/16in across, while the seatback-to-seatback legroom was around 70cm/30in. Admittedly, ancient Romans were both slimmer and shorter than modern people – a typical Roman was about 165cm/5ft 5in tall. But even so most spectators would have been packed in as tightly as passengers on a cheap flight today. Nonetheless, almost everyone got a reasonable view of events due to the arena's oval shape and very steep rake. Roman architects knew very well what they were doing when they designed the amphitheatre.

The *ambulacria* also offered a chance for non-elite spectators to stretch their legs in the often lengthy intervals between acts. The labyrinthine structure was so large that they could walk miles inside the amphitheatre, keeping out of the rain or the sun.

THE SUN AND THE RAIN

The Colosseum's awning, the *velarium*, offered some if not complete protection from Rome's volatile weather, but heavy rain would have penetrated the canvas quite swiftly, showering the audience below. The Romans lacked any form of waterproof clothing or umbrellas, although parasols, so lovingly mentioned by Ovid, might have offered some protection. In ancient Rome, however, only women used parasols and the only women in the amphitheatre, apart from the Vestal Virgins, were those sequestered at the very top, who were already partly sheltered from the elements. Paradoxically, senators in their prime seats on the *podium* would have been the most exposed. There is no mention in ancient sources of 'rain stopping play' and the amphitheatre was well designed to get rid of any water entering the *cavea*. Roman spectators must have accepted rain or sun with the stoical endurance they so admired in soldiers and in gladiators.

RIGID SEGREGATION

In the relatively easy-going later Republic, the different classes at times intermingled in the theatre, circus and amphitheatre. Attending a *munus*, knights and senators might rub shoulders with ordinary citizens when coming and going. Women too might brush against men as they made their way to their seats. This is revealed in a tale about Lucius Cornelius Sulla (138–78BC), who later became the most brutal dictator in Roman history. Sulla met his future wife Valeria when she walked behind where he was seated and removed a piece of fluff from his cloak. He was startled by this move but it led to a flirtatious exchange and in due course to marriage. 'He [Sulla] was seduced by her graceful looks and airs, through which disgraceful and shameful passions are aroused,' wrote the historian Plutarch priggishly.

This intermingling of men and women in the theatre and arena continued into the first years of Augustus's new empire after 27BC. The poet Ovid (43BC–AD17) in his *Ars Amatoria* ('The Art of Love') advised young men to use the chances offered by the arena to chat up young women who otherwise could be hard to meet. 'You yourself should hold her parasol above her/And with it clear a way through the crowd' [to her seat].

But as Augustus established his neo-conservative regime ever more firmly, he tried to restore the full rigour of old social divisions. Senators and knights were now allocated special seating areas in the auditorium and women, except for the Vestal Virgins, were totally segregated from men. The emperor also banished Ovid into miserable exile on the Black Sea – then anything but a holiday resort – offended by his erotic frivolity.

▲ *Ovid discourses on love in his* Ars Amatoria, *urging young men to chat up young women in the theatre. (Alamy)*

▼ *The seating in the amphitheatre at Verona, which has survived far better than that in the Colosseum, gives some idea of the original seating arrangements.*

THE RANKED SEATING SYSTEM

By the time the Colosseum was built, rigid social and sexual segregation in the arena was the accepted order of the day. It was indeed built into the structure itself. Unlike a modern football match or opera for example, where the best seats may be expensive but anyone who can scrape the money together can usually buy one, in Rome the best seats were only released to the elite.

THE PODIUM

The most desirable seats were on the *podium*, the lowest level closest to the arena and near the shorter axis. These were kept for the emperor and his courtiers and for the most important senators, the immensely wealthy upper aristocracy. The emperor and his entourage entered on the arena's south side on the short axis of the arena, through a triumphal arch bearing a bronze statue of a *quadriga,* four-horse chariot, which led to the *pulvinar,* the imperial box, adorned with coloured marbles and cushions. This part of the Colosseum has since vanished. Here the emperor, his courtiers and some very select guests watched the games, at times reclining on couches.

▼ *An unusually well-preserved section of the Colosseum, this is part of the original ceiling in the emperor's box, which would have been plastered and decorated in vivid colours. (Alamy)*

Across the arena on the opposite side sat the leading magistrates such as the consuls, who sometimes officially were giving the games. Near them sat the Arval Brethren – priests of an ancient order whose membership had become as much a badge of social status as a religious duty by AD80 – foreign ambassadors and similar dignitaries, and the Vestal Virgins. The rest of the 600 or so senators sat elsewhere on the *podium* on the seven rows of *subsellia*. These were individual ivory seats with backs, specially reserved for them. Some of the most important senators may also have had slave attendants crouched beside them or their adolescent sons near them. That the Senate sat directly opposite the emperor, each power block looking across the arena at the other, was symbolic and revealing of the tensions between them.

VIP spectators reached the *podium* via a tunnel, once richly decorated with stucco, leading to the innermost

ambulacrum. From this passage 12 staircases led up directly through the *vomitoria* out to the *podium*. This rigid segregation ensured senators never risked coming into contact with the lower orders, which can be seen as a microcosm of Roman society.

There were probably about 2,000 spectators in total in this most exclusive part of the auditorium. That foreign ambassadors or visitors, such as Herod Agrippa II, a protégé of the emperor Claudius and a future ruler of Judaea, sat on the *podium* near the senators indicates that nationality was less important than class. Class became increasingly more important in Rome during the imperial period, as senators, who formed in reality an almost hereditary aristocracy, acquired ever more privileges and wealth.

This was partly in exchange for the continuing decline of their power. Under the Republic the Senate had governed the Roman state, gerrymandering the electoral system so that it could usually get its favoured candidates elected to major offices such as consul or tribune. With Augustus's final assumption of supreme power by 27BC, the Senate lost all real power, but the emperor co-opted its members as administrators of the new state to disguise the brute reality of his military regime. It is perhaps significant that in the motto of the Roman state, *Senatus populusque Romanus* ('the Roman senate and people'), Senate came before people.

▲ *The neoclassical bronze* quadriga *on the roof of Banco de Bilbao in Madrid, Spain, was sculpted by Higinio de Basterra.*

▼ *The amphitheatre at El Jem, Tunisia, the empire's last new amphitheatre built in* AD235. *Seating 35,000, it is among the largest outside Italy. The* cavea *is unusually well preserved.*

VESTAL VIRGINS

Women were usually kept well away from the games, high up and so unable to see the gory details of combat or, equally important, to make eye contact with any good-looking gladiators. But one small group enjoyed prime views from seats right on the *podium*: the Vestal Virgins.

The six Vestals were an atypical group of women, however. Chosen between the ages of eight and ten from aristocratic families, they spent their next 30 years tending the sacred fire of the goddess Vesta in her circular temple on the edge of the Forum. This was considered a great honour but it was also a great burden, for they took a vow of chastity. If they broke it, they faced the draconian punishment of being buried alive – an old Roman penalty that had been allowed to lapse but which Domitian gleefully revived.

The Vestals enjoyed wide respect but by the time they had finished their sacerdotal duties, they were considered too old for marriage. Seeing the visceral thrills of the arena close up may have been some compensation for missing out on a normal life. There are tales of Vestals getting so carried away by the games that they stood up and cried out for or against individual gladiators. However, there are no records of Vestals running off with gladiators.

▲ *Statue of a Vestal Virgin, one of the young women from noble families who, from the age of eight, spent their lives tending the sacred fire of the goddess Vesta.*

▼ *Detail of the seating in the amphitheatre in Pula, Croatia. Its arena, which is broadly similar to the Colosseum's, has much better preserved seating.*

MAENIANUM PRIMUM

Immediately above the senators sat the knights or equestrians on the *maenianum primum* (first balcony) in the *ima cavea*, the lowest or best section of the *cavea* proper. Knights reached their reserved tiers of seating through their own inner *ambulacrum* that also kept them clear of the lower classes. Although they were only aristocrats of the second rank, knights were often very wealthy and could hold important posts such as Prefect of the elite Praetorian Guards. But, because there were about 20,000 knights in the Empire, the majority did not have individually reserved seats.

Despite this the most important knights – those to whom the emperor had granted the honour of an *equus publicus* or ceremonial horse, for instance – sat in special areas marked out for them. At one point there was also a block of ignominious seats for knights who had gone bankrupt. Where you sat, and were seen, in the Colosseum was a very public indicator of your status in society. In total the *ima cavea* may have had about 11,700 seats.

▼ *Although there is today no original seating extant in the Colosseum, a small area of the* maenianum primum *(first balcony) that was reserved for the* equites *(knights) was restored in the 1930s. The limited size of the seats shows that, even for these wealthy men, the seating was uncomfortably cramped if offering a good view.*

THE COLOSSEUM'S DRESS CODE

Roman citizens in the Colosseum had to wear a toga. This might seem too obvious to need stating but by AD80 the majority of Romans did *not* wear togas on a daily basis. This was because the archetypal Roman garment was heavy and awkward to wear, difficult to put on – it consisted of 6m/20ft of heavy wool that required careful folding – and expensive to keep clean, coming only in white.

By the end of the Republic many Roman citizens had abandoned the toga in favour of the simpler, more comfortable Greek *chiton,* the tunic worn by almost everyone around the Mediterranean. But Augustus, as part of his moral rearmament, ordered Roman citizens once more to wear togas when in the city's main public areas, such as the Forum or amphitheatre. This was to show that they were full citizens, for no one else could wear a toga. Domitian and other emperors later reiterated Augustus's sartorial commands. So, the mandatory wearing of togas in the better seats of the Colosseum reveals the high status of gladiatorial games in Roman public life, while the fact that a majority of spectators *did* wear togas underlines the relatively elite profile of much of the audience.

▲ *Modern visitors in two of the upper annular galleries, now broken and open to the sky. Originally these* ambulacria *would have provided areas sheltered from the sun or rain where spectators from the* media cavea *(middle tiers) could have strolled in the intervals between acts, buying snacks.*

MAENIANUM SECUNDUM

Above the *ima cavea* was the *media cavea* or *maenianum secundum* (second balcony), this had 19 rows of marble benches. Here sat full Roman citizens from what can be called the middle classes, those who had enough money to afford a toga, the badge of Roman respectability. These were men like retired centurions – soldiers of huge experience and solid wealth – or procurators, magistrates (officials) from the provincial cities. Soldiers on active duty also had blocks of seats reserved for them, as had some upper-class boys sitting with their tutors. There were probably about 24,000 places in this section. This section, which, like the rows higher up, had to be reached by vertiginously steep stairways in the arcaded outer galleries.

Today most tourists make use of the lifts recently installed. These, though so restricted in number that there are often long queues, spare modern visitors an exhausting climb. (See p146 for details of visiting the Colosseum today). When the amphitheatre was actually functioning as an amphitheatre, however, and was packed with spectators, every member of the audience had to climb the steep and often risky stairways, poorer citizens having to climb the furthest. Roman spectators never made use of the sort of elevators that brought wild beasts up from the depths of the *hypogeum* to the arena's surface. There were not nearly enough of these lifts. Anyway, being arduously winched upwards by slaves turning capstans, they were much too slow to be used like modern elevators to ferry human passengers. The distance from the *hypogeum* to the arena floor was also only about 8m/25ft, a manageable distance compared to that between the entrances and the higher seating in the *cavea*. Lifting tens of thousands of spectators to the amphitheatre's heights within a few minutes was far beyond Roman technology.

Poorer spectators' arduous ascent to their designated seating perhaps 30m/100ft above ground level underlines how hard life was even for free citizens in ancient Rome. The disabled or the merely elderly citizen certainly would not have been able to attend the games. But then few ordinary Roman citizens reached a respectable old age in a city notorious for its periodic outbreaks of plague, malaria, cholera and fire and the general malnutrition of its often under-employed or unemployed citizens.

SUMMA CAVEA

Above the *media cavea* rose the area known as the *summa cavea*, the superstructure. Here, about 11,000 definitely less important Romans, such as non-citizens – who initially made up a substantial part of the still-growing population – and foreigners, sat on wooden benches. These seats were probably not reserved but were taken on a first-come first-served basis. However, tokens for seats were still given out free of charge.

▲ *Part of the annular gallery running around the Colosseum at ground level. These were used to give the swarms of spectators access to the* cavea. *The bare brick structure now looks majestically imposing, as most the amphitheatre's interior surfaces were decorated, often with frescoes.*

This upper part of the Colosseum, because it was mostly built of wood to save weight, was badly damaged in the fire caused by the lightning strike of AD217. Such rebuilding after recurrent fire was common practice across the imperial city. Roman firefighting techniques, lacking the power to lift water any height, were utterly inadequate to deal with the repeated conflagrations, often started by the oil lamps used for lighting and charcoal braziers used for heating.

SUMMUM MAENIANUM

Above the *summa cavea* was the *summum maenianum in ligneis,* a high wooden gallery. Here, there was standing room only for perhaps 10,000 spectators, mostly slaves or freedmen. And right at the very top, some 45m/144ft above the arena, tucked beneath the portico that ran round the summit of the *cavea*, sat the women. Probably mostly upper-class, they were a long way from the action but they were also sheltered from the sun and rain more effectively than was the rest of the crowd. A barrier prevented them from falling into the *cavea* and shielded them from the eyes of men below, creating a sort of purdah. These ladies probably had high-backed chairs, giving them much the same comfort as senators down below.

GLADITORIAL GLAMOUR

Despite the best efforts of officialdom to keep women spectators and gladiators apart, some noble women, succumbed to the gladiators' potent mixture of glamour, fine physique, danger and roughness. Some women somehow got to meet them – not, obviously, in the actual arena but before or after games in the Ludus Magnus. A few women even had affairs with gladiators – something especially shocking in a society as rigidly stratified as Rome's. These women were known as *inamoratae,* enamoured women. Juvenal, the greatest satirical poet of the empire, scornfully immortalised one such woman:

What was the youthful charm that so enchanted Eppia?
What did she see that made it worth being called
  gladiatrix?
Her 'darling boy' had begun shaving long before…
besides, he was frightfully ugly.
But gladiators look better to women than an adonis.
This is what she preferred to her children, country and
  husband,
The gladiator's sword is what these women adore.
                              Juvenal, *Satires,* CAD110

CONVENIENCES AND AMENITIES

The lack of seating space made breaks in the day's entertainment – and a day at the games meant literally that – essential. The Colosseum was well supplied with one necessary convenience; toilets (bathrooms), an area in which the Romans often excelled. Traces have been found that indicate plumbing for latrines in several areas inside the structure of the Colosseum along with 20 fountains that supplied drinking water. In fact facilities then were probably better than they are today.

LUNCHTIME REFRESHMENTS

Other forms of refreshment were, however, lacking. Senators and knights often retired for a midday break, with lunch and siesta, in part to avoid the noontide mass executions whose lack of finesse they deplored. (The cruelty involved hardly disturbed them.) Less exalted spectators, however, generally stayed put. This may have been partly to keep their seats or because their homes were too far away to reach easily. Many brought lunch with them, as traces of nuts, shellfish – which the Romans particularly loved – sausages, also a Roman speciality, olive stones and fruit pips have been found clogging the drains of the amphitheatre. Such snacks were also sold by vendors, who appeared in the *cavea* during breaks in the performances.

OCCASIONAL GIFTS

Spectators could sometimes hope for free refreshments from the emperor himself. These were the ancient equivalent of a Big Mac and Coke, not a full meal, but they were still handed out free to spectators, though only as a special treat. At times emperors such as Nero or Domitian ate publicly in the Colosseum to show that the emperor at heart was really a man of the people. The food and wine in the imperial box were presumably far better than the snacks offered to the populace.

PERFUMES, PRESENTS AND PRIZES

The emperor's largesse was not restricted to handing out the odd snack. At various times on hot summer afternoons the sweating crowds, jammed together on their benches, would be refreshed by a sudden sprinkling of perfume from huge dispensers above the *cavea*. (How these worked is unknown.) Although the Romans were unusually clean by ancient standards – their free public baths were among the City's wonders – this perfuming must have been welcomed by many, as deodorants were unknown and perfumes very expensive.

Even more welcome was the distribution of tokens for presents or prizes. These were handed – or thrown – to the crowds at intervals between the acts. The crowd – not the senators or knights, obviously – could fight for these tokens, for some of the prizes were worth having. The very lucky might win a large sum of money or even a villa outside Rome. Most prizes, however, were for modest sums or gifts. As with the snacks and the perfume spraying, these distributions were seldom advertised beforehand. The deity to whom gladiators prayed most often was Tyche, the Greek name for Fortuna, the goddess of chance. The audience must have prayed to her at times too.

AUDIENCE REACTION

What Roman audiences most wanted to see was a good fight, with plenty of gore, human and/or animal, at the end. Death was definitely part of the ritual – this aspect of the original funeral rites remained long after the games had become primarily entertainment – although by no means every gladiator had to die in a contest, even if he lost. What every gladiator was expected to do was to display *virtus* to encourage others to fight and die bravely.

Virtus was a crucial Roman quality (the English word 'virtue' comes from it, of course). It meant courage, manliness, integrity and ability, the very qualities that had created and sustained the empire. For the Roman ruling classes chose to see the games not just as entertainment for the masses – though the *munera* were, along with the races, Rome's supreme entertainment – but also as a way of teaching the Roman people fortitude endurance, manliness and courage, or *virtus.*

Cicero (106–43BC), one of the greatest writers of the late Republic and a notably humane man, was voicing the views of many Roman aristocrats when he praised the way the contests encouraged *virtus* in young spectators. Seneca, the Stoic philosopher and statesman who for a while served as an advisor to Nero, stayed on in the arena once for the lunchtime show. He was appalled at the acts' crudity, which required no skill and offered no morally uplifting displays of *virtus,* unlike the *munera.* The brutality of the gladiatorial games later on, however, did not really worry this great exponent of Stoicism with its high-minded beliefs in the brotherhood of men.

> Now all subtlety is cast aside and we have murder pure and simple. The fighters have no protective armour, their whole bodies are exposed to the blows… This is what most people prefer to regular fights and it is obvious why… Why bother with armour? Why with skills? All these just delay death. In the morning men are thrown to the lions and bears. At midday they are thrown to the spectators themselves… In the end every fighter dies… 'Kill him, beat him, burn him!' the crowds cry.
>
> Seneca, *Epistulae Morales ad Lucilium,* CAD60

▶ *Cicero, the politician, lawyer and philosopher, believed that the* munera *encouraged Roman* virtus, *meaning 'courage' or 'manliness'. (Alamy)*

Attitudes of the emperors

Marcus Aurelius, the philosopher-emperor, wrote in his *Meditations* that he found the *munera* 'boring' – an unusual reaction – but he still gave and attended games, as part of his imperial duties. At first he dealt with his correspondence during them. Later, realising this was creating a bad impression, he dictated to secretaries or discussed affairs of state with his ministers, so that the crowd might think they were talking about the games. His lack of interest was countered by the manic enthusiasm of his successor – and supposed son – Commodus, who took part in many games himself.

More usually, emperors at least feigned to enjoy the spectacles that they were putting on, to please the people. This applied to the first Christian emperor Constantine as much as to Marcus Aurelius or to another emperor strongly interested in philosophy, Gallienus, who reigned AD253–268. Even Theodosius I, who effectively banned public performance of all pagan rites in AD391, did not dare put an end to the *munera*, despite being a most devout Christian.

Individual Christians' attitudes to the games could be markedly ambivalent, however. St Augustine in his *Confessions*, around AD398, describes how Alypius,

▼ *The Arch of Constantine in the Forum Romanum near the Colosseum. Through his long reign Constantine increasingly favoured Christianity and had little enthusiasm for the* munera.

▲ *Carving from the obelisk of Theodosius I in the hippodrome of Constantinople (Istanbul). Theodosius banned all public pagan worship, with which the games were linked.*

a young Christian, had finally succumbed to the pleas of some pagan friends and gone with them to the amphitheatre. Alypius was determined to keep his eyes shut so that he could still claim to have *seen* nothing, but he proved unable to keep his eyes closed throughout the roars of the performance. The moment he peeped through his fingers, he was hooked. 'When he saw the blood it was as though he had drunk deeply of savage passions,'

▲ *Despite Christianity becoming the official religion of the empire, pagan sentiments and beliefs died hard, as this sarcophagus from around AD500, showing Greco-Roman myth, found in Istanbul, attests.*

S. AVGVSTINVS

wrote Augustine. Alypius for a while became a devotee of the games, dragging others along with him until he was finally saved by his conscience. He later became a bishop.

It took a long time for the Roman populace to turn against the games but by the year AD400 there were signs of this happening. It was also becoming harder to find gladiators. Romans were now being made captive by German invaders more frequently than vice-versa. Finally, the *munera's* close ties with the public performance of pagan rites meant that both went out of fashion together as Christianity became almost universally if perhaps superficially accepted across all classes. Economic decline combined with these religious and social factors to bring an end to the *munera*, probably by around AD433. In the wake of invasions and recurrent civil wars, the once-sophisticated economy of the western half of the Roman Empire contracted. In some places it may have almost collapsed, ending the inflows of taxes and tributes that had given the capital the wealth to stage its lavish games.

◄ *St Augustine writing, from a 19th-century fresco in Turin. Augustine (AD354–430), the most eloquent of the 'Fathers of the Church', was one of the greatest opponents of the* munera, *because he felt the games corrupted spectators.*

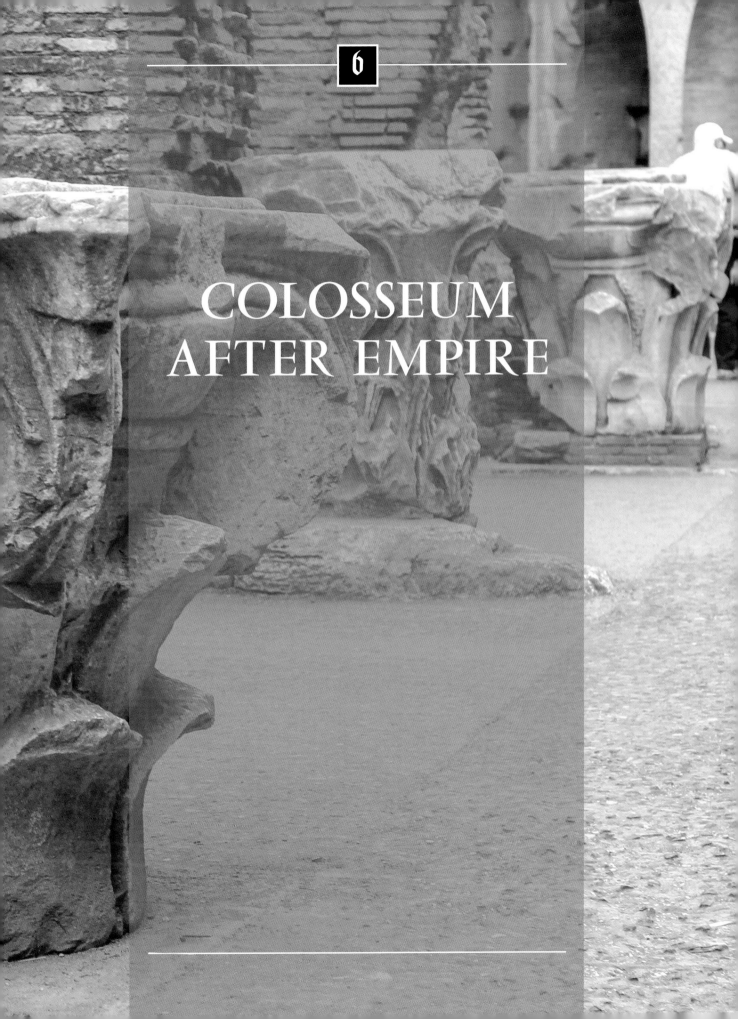

6

COLOSSEUM AFTER EMPIRE

THE DECLINE OF ROME

When a German mercenary general called Odoacer deposed the emperor Romulus Augustulus in 476, he officially put an end to the Western Roman Empire. The imperial insignia were sent to the emperor in Constantinople to signify the reunion of the Eastern and Western Empires. In theory the various Germanic tribes who had taken over almost all the Western Empire were now vassals of the East Roman Emperor. In practice they were totally independent.

Yet urban life continued in an attenuated way in Rome itself. The aqueducts still supplied abundant clean water for the baths, the Senate still sat and deliberated, chariot races were still run in the Circus Maximus and in the Colosseum *venationes,* at times combined with boxing matches or other non-lethal contests, were still staged, albeit on a much reduced scale.

▼ *The Church of Hagia Sofia in Constantinople, capital of the Eastern Empire. It was built between AD532 and 537 by the architects Isidore and Anthemius for Emperor Justinian as the power base of the Romans moved east, away from Rome.*

THE LAST GAMES

One of the final events in the Colosseum was held in AD523 under Theodoric, king of the Ostrogoths occupying Italy. (The Ostrogoths were cousins of the Visigoths who had sacked Rome in 410. Like the Visigoths they had converted to Christianity before 400 but unfortunately both had become Arians, a sect considered heretical by most Romans.) Despite this handicap, Theodoric ruled Italy from 493 to 526 with surprising moderation and sagacity from Ravenna, which had been the last capital of the Western Empire. He did so partly by enlisting the support of Roman nobles such as Cassiodorus (c490–585), who was a senator and consul

▲ *This mosaic from San Vitale in Ravenna, Italy, shows the emperor Justinian flanked by his courtiers. Under Justinian large parts of the Western Empire were recovered by the East Romans, although their reconquest proved costly.*

▼ *The sack of Rome in AD546 by the Ostrogoths, trying to regain their kingdom from the East Romans, left the city in ruins. Here, Hadrian's Mausoleum falls to the invaders. (Getty)*

before becoming a renowned Benedictine monk. In his ministerial role Cassiodorus helped organise what may have been the very last games in the arena in 523.

King Theodoric tried to preserve both the fabric and the customs of the Eternal City. Although the king personally found *venationes* distasteful, he ordered repairs to the Colosseum after it was damaged by yet another earthquake in 508. By that time, procuring enough exotic wild beasts from around the Mediterranean for a decent *venatio* must have become extremely difficult for the impoverished city.

The real end of the ancient world for Italy came in the 540s. The long wars, between the East Roman or Byzantine armies attempting to reconquer Italy and the Ostrogoths trying to retain it, snuffed out the last glimmers of urban life in Rome. In the siege of 546 the city's aqueducts along with its grain supplies were cut off, leading to its near total depopulation. According to the Byzantine historian Procopius, who was an eyewitness of the siege, although one prone to exaggeration, there were only 500 inhabitants left in Rome by the year 547, a city whose population had once passed the 1 million mark.

Both the Senate and people disappeared, leaving only the

The first hunter, trusting only to a brittle pole, runs onto the mouths of the beasts and seems, so eagerly does he charge, almost to want the death he hopes to avoid… The man's bent limbs are tossed into the air like flimsy bits of clothing by the powerful leap of his body and the animal shoots past underneath before the hunter's body can fall back. Another hunter, making use of four small panels rotating around a central pole and keeping close to his animal adversary, escapes not by running away or keeping his distance but follows his pursuers, so as to avoid the mouths of the bears. Another man, stretching out on his stomach on a low bar, teases a deadly beast. Unless he took such risks, he would not survive. Another man fighting a ferocious animal protects himself with a portable reed wall, much like a hedgehog. Just as the hedgehog when danger looms rolls itself into a ball and is defended by its own spines so the man, protected by the wicker wall, is strengthened by frail reeds. In the arena other men protected by three small doors dare to goad the wild animals awaiting them, hiding themselves behind latticed gates, at times showing their faces and sometimes their backs so it seems miraculous that they can escape the claws and teeth of the lions.

Cassiodorus, in a letter to King Theodoric, AD523

Pope to preside. The grand imperial palaces on the Palatine Hill and the immense domed public baths slowly collapsed through neglect while the Forum itself became a pasture for cows, the 'Campo Vaccino', as it remained known until the 19th century. Very few important buildings survived even half intact. One that did was the Pantheon, which had the good fortune to be turned into a church in 608, so safeguarding it. Another was the Colosseum.

Although the amphitheatre had no obvious alternative uses, being in fact totally redundant, its massive solidity ensured its survival. The statues that filled its arches and its marble and gilt decorations proved tempting to robbers, however. One of these robbers wore the imperial purple: Constans II, a Byzantine emperor, who briefly visited the city in 663 and stripped it of yet more treasures, including the Pantheon's roof of gilded tiles. (Constans was murdered soon after this in his bath.) The rise of the Arab empire then threatened Rome with seaborne raiders who were no respecters either of pagan monuments or of Christian churches. In 846 Arab pirates plundered the Vatican, carrying off even sacred items from the high altar of St Peter's Basilica. The Colosseum itself was ignored by the Arabs but in 847 it was harmed by another earthquake.

▼ *The* Campo Vacino *or 'Cow Pasture', as the Forum had become known, painted by the British artist J.M.W. Turner in 1835. By then many of Rome's ruins had been neglected.*

▲ *On Christmas Day AD800 the Frankish king Charlemagne was crowned by the pope in St Peter's Basilica, supposedly reviving the Roman Empire in the west.*

▶ *The Venerable Bede (AD673–735), eminent Anglo-Saxon historian, hailed the Colosseum as a symbol of Rome's strength, overlooking its bloody past. Bede was one of the first people to call the amphitheatre by its present name. (Alamy)*

THE PILGRIMS' REPORT

Despite such vicissitudes, Rome's status as the Eternal City, now seen in a Christian light as its pagan past faded into the mist of legend, grew steadily. In the early Middle Ages (or 'Dark Ages'), more and more pilgrims from across Europe began making the arduous, even dangerous journey to the city, the holiest in western Christendom where St Peter had been martyred and was buried. They were seeking the total remission of their sins that such a pilgrimage offered. Rome attracted more worldly-minded visitors too.

Charlemagne, the first 'Holy Roman Emperor' who ruled most of Western Europe, was crowned in St Peter's Basilica on Christmas Day 800 by the pope. For centuries afterwards most Holy Roman emperors – who in fact were usually German kings, not Romans at all – wanted a papal coronation in Rome to consecrate their power. Some, like the idealistic young Otto III (983–1002), even tried to rule from the Palatine Palace like a real Caesar. This proved a mistake. A rioting mob forced Otto to flee the city precipitously. Rome in decay may have seemed majestic but it was also anarchic.

While all other ancient buildings fell into ruin – except for the churches, maintained by donations from the endless stream of pilgrims – the Colosseum appeared almost immortal, as befitted the Eternal City. In fact, it was the building that impressed visiting pilgrims more than any other in Rome, even St Peter's. Rising only marginally damaged over the now overgrown Forum, its majestic tiers of columns and arches awed visitors from the primitive north who had never seen a building remotely comparable. These pilgrims, however, had no idea about what had once taken place inside the arena.

Reports by pilgrims coming back from Rome led the Venerable Bede of Northumberland, one of the 8th century's most learned men, to hail the amphitheatre as an emblem of the Christian city's enduring strength and greatness:

> While stands the Coliseum, Rome shall stand;
> When falls the Coliseum Rome shall fall;
> And when Rome falls – the world falls.
> The Venerable Bede, c730, trans. by Lord Byron

Bede definitely meant by these lines the amphitheatre, not the statue of the Sun God, whose pagan nudity would have appalled him had he known of it. (If not carried off long before by the Vandals when they sacked Rome in 455, the statue had probably been melted down by then, the fate of most ancient bronze statues. Bronze was a highly valued material.)

> The Colosseum was the Temple of the Sun, of marvellous greatness and beauty, composed of many different vaulted chambers, all covered in a heaven of gilded bronze, where thunders and lightnings and gleaming fires were made, and from which rain fell through silver tubes.
> *Mirabilia Urbis Romae* (*The Marvels of Rome, Guidebook for Pilgrims*), c1100

QUARRY, FORTRESS, GARDENS, BULL RING

The amphitheatre had survived the fall of the empire that had created it, but the uses found for it in the following centuries were seldom glorious. Its chief role for the next 1,200 years was in fact as a quarry. Many of Rome's medieval, Renaissance and baroque buildings are built at least in part of masonry taken from the Colosseum. This contributes to the charm of Rome today but it has not helped preserve the fabric of the amphitheatre.

A TEMPLE TO THE SUN?

An irritating thing about the Colosseum today is our total ignorance of the architects and builders involved. (The names of some earlier and several later Roman architects *are* known.) The Middle Ages thought it knew better. Medieval writers were certain that Virgil, the great Latin poet cast by Dante as his guide through hell in his epic poem *Inferno*, had actually designed the amphitheatre. This belief was not shaken by the fact that Virgil had died in 19BC, nearly a century before the Colosseum was built. Virgil himself was credited with magical powers, so he was presumably thought fully capable of erecting such a structure a century after his death. Many medieval writers also thought that the amphitheatre had once been a gold-roofed temple to the sun, dominated by a statue either of Jupiter or of the Sun God in the arena's centre. No one realised that it had been built as a place of competitive slaughter.

▼ *This mosaic held in the Bardo National Museum, Tunis, shows Virgil (centre), writing* The Aeneid, *inspired by the muses, Clio and Melpomene.*

Around the year 1000 economic and social life in Western Europe began to revive. Powerful new city-states now emerged in Italy: Venice, Pisa, Amalfi and Genoa growing rich through trade across the Mediterranean. Rome, however, had only a small part in the general quickening. It had never been a trading or manufacturing city but a centre of power and consumption. But while it now lacked a mighty empire to support it in luxury, in the pope it had a figure to whom all Christendom paid tribute. This tribute was both spiritual and financial.

Although medieval urban life in Rome never rivalled that of the imperial centuries, new buildings began to appear in the city where only trees had sprouted among the ruins. The papacy, after a period when it was a mere plaything of the local nobility, regained its confidence under a series of vigorous reformist popes. And it began to build again. The new buildings, whether religious or secular – churches were grander and more numerous than private houses – needed cut stone and iron. The most obvious source of such materials in Rome were the old buildings still rising splendid if ruinous above the city. The Colosseum now faced even worse threats to its existence than earthquakes or lightning strikes.

MATERIAL PLUNDER

Among the earliest items to have been looted from the amphitheatre were the 300 tons of iron clamps used to hold the arches' stone blocks together – stealing metal was always easier than mining and smelting it. Archaeologists have determined that the Colosseum's lower, more accessible tiers lost their metal supports first, while the upper tiers were pillaged later. It is a tribute to the skills of the unknown builders that the amphitheatre has survived these thefts, although parts of its facade have been disfiguringly pockmarked. (Attempts at restoring some of the iron clamps in the 19th century proved unsuccessful visually and redundant structurally.)

Even more damaging both structurally and aesthetically was the removal of some of the travertine buttresses forming the arches and vaults. Marble from the Colosseum's seats and façade proved when burnt to produce the perfect material for mortar, while the lead pipes and drains also were equally useful and were removed too. This looting, which was often sanctioned by the popes themselves, finally produced the half-wrecked appearance the amphitheatre has today. Although the Colosseum did not collapse, being massively over-engineered like many Roman public buildings, the

▶ *Portrait of Gregory VII, pope from 1073 to 1085, who was exiled from Rome after his Norman allies sacked the city. He never returned to the city and died in exile in Salerno. (Getty)*

cavea's interior was exposed to the elements. Gradually the arena and *hypogeum* filled with earth in which there soon seeded exuberantly growing plants.

A NEW DWELLING FOR ROME'S RESIDENTS

As the papacy's prestige grew in the 11th century, it started to challenge the political primacy of the Holy Roman Emperor. This could be risky. The Emperor had the largest army in Europe and did not hesitate to use it. So Pope Gregory VII (r1073–85) discovered when he had to flee from advancing imperial troops in 1084. Gregory turned for help to Robert Guiscard, leader of the Normans who were then conquering Sicily from the Arabs with papal blessing. The Normans responded en force but behaved so brutally in Rome that its citizens turned on them. Angered, the Normans then sacked the city. The ensuing massacre was the worst since the Vandals' 600 years earlier and Gregory VII was forced into exile. He left a city in renewed chaos.

The Frangipani and Annibaldi families

The chaos led Roman noble families to convert many of Rome's monuments into forts. Nearly every extant ancient building was now seen as a potential castle – even triumphal arches sprouted turrets and battlements. The powerful Colonna dynasty took over the ruins on the Capitol Hill and in 1144 the aristocratic Frangipani family got papal permission to occupy and fortify the Colosseum.

The immense circuit of the *cavea* proved too large for their purposes so they occupied only 13 arches on two tiers at the eastern end of the amphitheatre. Here, they constructed a fortress-palace, complete with towers and battlements. Looking down on the overgrown arena the Frangipani family lived and entertained – Pope Lucius II was one of their guests – until forced to hand over their castle to the Annibaldi family in the early 13th century. The Annibaldi entertained Petrarch in their castle when he visited Rome for his 'coronation' as a poet in 1337. They sold up in the 1360s to monks who may have built a small church there that has long since been demolished.

Homes for the common Roman

Rome's ordinary citizens had meanwhile been colonising the lower slopes of the amphitheatre's interior. Huts nestled into the massive tiers provided relatively secure if insalubrious homes within the arena perimeter. Other even poorer Romans used the tunnels as caves, with families squalling in them for generations. Traces of animal stalls, haylofts and human dwellings, some dating back to the late 6th century, have been found. There also survive legal records of ownership referring to gardens, courtyards, small houses and boundaries, with owners variously listed as blacksmiths, shoemakers and lime-pit workers. The Colosseum had become in effect a little city within the city.

A HAVEN FOR FLORA

All this small-scale burrowing, coupled with the use of other parts of the amphitheatre as a huge manure tip, aggravated the structural damage caused by bigger depredations. (Manure can be highly acidic, eating into stone.) But the profusion of small gardens, abundant natural fertiliser and general neglect in what proved to be the *cavea's* unusually benign microclimate allowed an extraordinary profusion of plants to flourish for centuries. In 1643 Domenico Panaroli, a Professor of Botany and Anatomy at La Sapienza, the university of Rome, made the first proper study of the amphitheatre's flora. He listed a total of 337 different species of plants and flowers, some very rare. They must have arrived in the Colosseum as seeds in the fur of the exotic animals that had died in the amphitheatre more than a thousand years before. Sadly, subsequent restoration and cleaning programmes have scoured clean this cornucopia.

BULLFIGHTING

On 3 September 1332 the amphitheatre unwittingly rediscovered its ancient role: a bullfight was staged in the arena, the first such spectacle for 800 years. It was held in honour of the Holy Roman Emperor Louis IV of Bavaria then visiting Rome – he had been crowned there six years earlier. (Bullfights, although famously Spanish, may have been partly Roman in origin. Bullrings certainly echo amphitheatres in their overall design, although none compares with the Colosseum.) The bullfight proved very popular with Romans, who crowded into the ruined *cavea* to see it. But it was a one-off and no one seems to have made the connection between this contest and its ancient precursors.

The Colosseum itself, however, remained the supreme emblem of the Eternal City in the European imagination. Following the examples of Frederick Barbarossa (r1152–90) and other Holy Roman Emperors, Louis had the Colosseum engraved on his imperial *bullae*, the grand seals used for official letters and documents, so identifying himself with the spirit of Rome. Meanwhile the actual building continued to suffer from neglect and depredation. A serious earthquake in 1349 caused parts of the west and south sides of the *cavea,* already weakened by the removal of much of its travertine, to collapse. This encouraged further opportunistic looting.

In 1382 the civil, as opposed to papal, government of Rome, the Capitoline Senate, realising at last that something must be done, gave three separate authorities responsibility for maintaining the building. Such division of powers did little to save the amphitheatre. Papal documents record frequent grants or sales of permits for quarrying up to the mid-17th century, a process described officially as *cavar marmi a Coliseo* (to quarry marble from the Colosseum). In nine months during 1452 under Pope Nicholas V, 2,522 cart loads of travertine were carried off to be burnt as lime for the rebuilding of St Peter's Basilica.

Two centuries later the process was still continuing. Much of the stone for the Palazzo Barberini, a baroque palace, came from the Colosseum. The process was authorised

▲ A fanciful map of Rome illustrating the geographical poem Dittamonto by the writer Fazio degli Uberti (1305–67). The Colosseum can just be made out in the centre of the city, as the most important of Rome's ancient monuments. (Getty)

◄ St Peter's Basilica was rebuilt in the 16th and 17th centuries, in part of stone looted from the Colosseum.

▲ *The Palazzo Barberini in Rome, built by Borromini and Bernini – a rare collaboration – partly of stone looted from the Colosseum, that too-accessible source of masonry.*

by Pope Urban VIII (r1623–44), himself a Barberini. This plundering led witty Romans to quip: '*Quod non fecerunt barbari, fecerunt Barberini*' ('What the barbarians never accomplished, the Barberini have').

▼ The Massacre of the Triumvirate *by Antoine Caron (1521–99), mingling memories of the Massacre of St Bartholomew's Eve with a fantasy of the Colosseum. (Alamy)*

SORCERY AND MAGIC

During the Middle Ages the unlit tunnels beneath the Colosseum after dark acquired a sinister reputation as a haunt of evil spirits and necromancers, despite the benign renown of Virgil, its supposed builder. This reputation lasted well into the Renaissance. In 1534 the sculptor and adventurer Benvenuto Cellini (1500–71), who had fallen helplessly in love with Angelica, a Sicilian girl, decided to use magic to win her heart. He had long been interested in black magic, admitting that 'throughout my life I have longed to see or learn something of this art'. A priest who professed knowledge of necromantic skills agreed to perform the requisite rites at night inside the arena. The first attempt having little effect, they returned the following night with two friends of Cellini's and a boy of 'unquestioned pure virginity', one of Cellini's assistants. The priest uttered 'awful incantations calling on a multitude of demons … soon the whole Colosseum was full of a hundredfold as many … I demanded to be reunited with Angelica.' Yet more demons continued to appear and proved beyond the powers of the priest to control. Cellini's companions were struck by panic, the boy crying out that 'a million of the fiercest men were swarming around and threatening us'. At this point one of Cellini's terrified friends lost control of his bowels. The resulting awful stench drove the devils off, although Cellini and his companions remained inside their protective magic circle until daybreak.

RENAISSANCE REVIVAL

Around the start of the 15th century the Renaissance, the rebirth of classical antiquity, began in Florence and quickly spread across Italy. What was reborn was a desire to explore the ancient world, especially of Rome, whose remains were then far more evident in Italy than they are today, and to emulate its artistic and architectural splendours. Sculpting, painting and building in the *maniera all'antica* (the ancient style) became almost mandatory.

When Florentine architects such as Brunelleschi, Alberti and Sangallo the Younger visited Rome to sketch its ancient monuments, the Colosseum was the building that most inspired them. Sangallo designed the Palazzo Farnese in Rome in 1515, whose facade of three superimposed orders of columns pay tribute to the amphitheatre. Earlier Alberti had published two influential books on Roman architecture. He dedicated them to Eugenius IV (who was pope from 1431 to 1447) who, filled with the new enthusiasm for antiquity, forbade further dismantling of the Colosseum. Sadly,

▼ *A map of Rome c1580 by Giacomo Lauro. Obsessed, like many Renaissance artists with visions of the city, Lauro reconstructed most of Rome's greatest monuments. (Alamy)*

Eugenius was a notably ineffectual pontiff and his decrees were ignored.

The amphitheatre now began appearing in Renaissance paintings as the archetypal image of Rome, and not just in works by Italian artists. When Pieter Bruegel the Elder, the leading Flemish artist of his day, stayed in Rome for two years between 1552 and 1554, he became obsessed by this edifice so unlike anything he had seen in the Netherlands. He painted at least four dramatic pictures in which its soaring mass dominates the scene. He called them all *The Tower of Babel*, presumably because such a title meant more to biblically minded buyers in northern Europe than classical allusions, but they all definitely show the Colosseum.

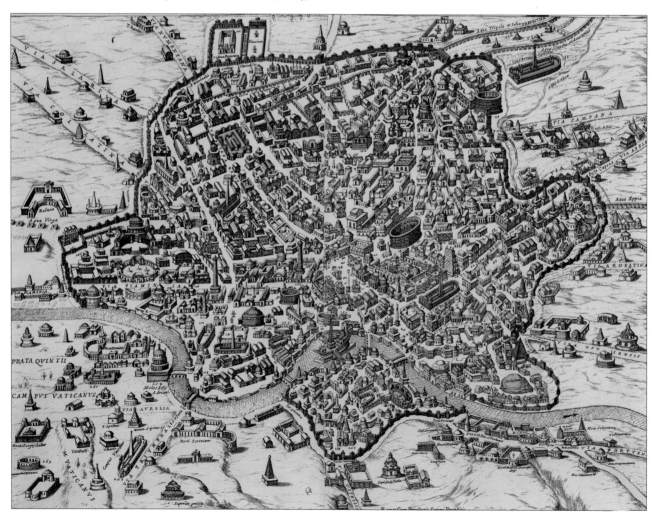

▶ *Reconstruction of the Colosseum c1570 by Antonio Lafreri. His vision of the amphitheatre with its cutaway section is notably accurate. (Alamy)*

▼ The Tower of Babel, *1563 by Pieter Bruegel the Elder. He painted three versions of the tower, all of which feature massive ruined structures inspired by his memories of the Colosseum.*

About this time the Church came to the gradual and belated realisation that the original function of the arena had been a killing field, at least according to time-honoured stories that most Romans still accepted as true. This had the paradoxical effect of turning a pagan amphitheatre into a site of Christian martyrdom. Condemned criminals had indeed been frequently executed in Rome's arena and Christians had often been seen as criminals, albeit ones of a special sort. (By refusing to sacrifice to the gods on whose protection Rome depended, they were thought to be endangering the safety of the whole empire.)

But to the popes and the Church these unknown victims were seen simply as martyrs. Services began to be held inside the amphitheatre as it assumed the role of a place of martyrdom. A large cross was erected on the north side of the arena and a small chapel of Santa Maria della Pietà al Colosseo built at the northeastern end. Other crucifixes were set up, turning the arena's interior into Stations of the Cross.

Both Pope Clement X in the 1670s and Pope Clement XI in the early 18th century wanted to build a church inside the Colosseum, but their plans came to nothing, perhaps fortunately. An earlier role for the Colosseum had proved equally abortive. In 1585 Pope Sixtus V had plans to convert it into a textile mill. The scheme drawn up by the pope's architect Domenico Fontana envisaged industrial machinery on the ground floor of the amphitheatre, with accommodation for workers on the upper floors. All this was part of a wider plan to tidy up the Forum. The project proved impractical, however, and died with Pope Sixtus in 1590. The amphitheatre's mixed uses – as garden, dwelling, shrine and above all quarry – continued.

RESTORATION AND EXCAVATION

In 1743 the Capitoline Senate made the first real attempt at protecting the Colosseum for more than a millennium. A law was passed forbidding further looting of the building and threatening to whip anyone found damaging the structure or who even left the amphitheatre's gates open after nightfall. In 1749 Pope Benedict XIV dedicated the Colosseum to the Passion of Jesus and declared it sanctified by the blood of its (presumed) Christian martyrs, finally safeguarding what remained.

Repairs started in the 1760s and soon proved they were vital to stop the outer walls collapsing. Further reinforcement was needed for the outer corridors and in the 1790s enclosure walls were built on the lower two levels between the arcades and the barrel vaults. After another earthquake in 1803 Pope Pius VII ordered the building of a vast triangular buttressing wall at the east end. It was not completed until 1820 and is still very visible. Further restoration went hand-in-hand with excavations, the latter often necessitating the former for digging threatened to undermine the structure.

18TH-CENTURY EXCAVATIONS

Like most of Italy, Rome fell to the French revolutionary armies in the 1790s, officially becoming part of Napoleon Bonaparte's empire in 1808. The French tricolour for a time flew over the Vatican as French soldiers swept away the ancient regime. Some also wanted to sweep away the more decayed southern half of the Colosseum to tidy it up but others, more enlightened, began excavating the arena. They dug deep into the earth still filling the arena to reveal vaulted chambers along the north side that had once held the lifts for wild animals.

Digging had in fact started in a spasmodic way in 1714 but only in 1791 did Carlo Lucangeli, an Italian engineer, begin excavating systematically. Lucangeli employed gangs of workers to clear the rubble blocking the *cavea's* upper vaults and then to excavate the lower levels. Officially employed from 1805, he uncovered the complex drainage system beneath the pavement and some vaulted tunnels that he took to be toilets and brothels. (They are in fact neither, although the Colosseum was well equipped with flushing lavatories, like most Roman buildings.) Lucangeli's teams also discovered the richly stuccoed imperial entrance corridor – a part of the amphitheatre that is now dated to Commodus's reign (AD180–192).

Lucangeli's book on the Colosseum, which included the first accurate drawing of the building as he thought it looked in its prime, was published in 1813, the year after his death. His drawing was based on the remarkably accurate cork model of the amphitheatre he had made. One version of the model still exists in the Colosseum and another is in the Académie des Beaux-Arts in Paris.

▲ *In the 17th and 18th centuries the Colosseum was increasingly used for services as the erroneous idea spread that many Christians had once been martyred there.*

▼ *Cut-away of the model archaeologist Carlo Lucangeli made of the Colosseum between 1790 and 1812. Lucangeli made the first systematic excavations of the amphitheatre. (Alamy)*

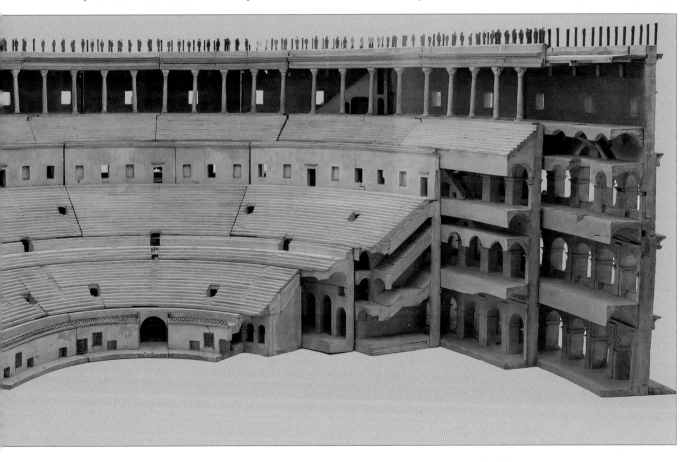

THE ARTIST'S ROMANTIC RUIN

The Colosseum's appeal was always far more than just archaeological. In the 18th century, Rome, long a mecca for aspiring young artists from across Europe, began to attract a new type of visitor: the Grand Tourist, who was often a rich aristocratic dilettante. At first these wealthy visitors came mainly from France and Britain. Later, Americans, such as Mark Twain and Henry James, and some Germans joined this new type of pilgrimage to admire ancient art and architecture.

The French liked to paint the Colosseum, often depicting it as poetically overgrown with trees and vines. The British preferred to measure its dimensions admiringly and then pilfer tiny bits of it to take home. Their admiration led to the erection of several buildings inspired by the amphitheatre in the British Isles, most notably in Bath.

EDWARD GIBBON

A Briton inspired in another way was the historian Edward Gibbon, author of the monumental *A History of the Decline and Fall of the Roman Empire*, published in six volumes. Gibbon was a serious scholar but he had a dramatic, even romantic streak, as his grandiloquent style reveals. He described the Colosseum as, 'An edifice that, had it been left to time and nature might perhaps have claimed an eternal duration… Whatever was precious, or portable, or profane, the statues of gods and heroes, and the costly ornaments of sculpture which were cast in brass, or overspread with leaves of silver and gold, became the first prey of conquest or fanaticism, of the avarice of the Barbarians or the Christians'.

WOLFGANG VON GOETHE

Wolfgang von Goethe, the German poet and dramatist, spent several life-changing months in Rome in 1786–87. The Colosseum was the ruin that moved him most and in his journal he jotted down his first impressions on 11 November:

In the evening we came upon the Colosseum when it was already twilight. When one looks at it everything else seems tiny: the edifice is so vast that one cannot hold the image of

▼ *Capriccio, 1735, by Giovanni Paolo Pannini. Pannini painted fantastical scenes of Rome. His depiction of the Colosseum is accurate, but other elements are invented. (Alamy)*

A ROMAN CIRCUS IN BATH

One of the finest post-Roman homages to the Colosseum is in Bath, southwest England. Bath, named Aquae Sulis at the time of the Roman Empire, had been a city of some importance during that period due to its thermal baths but its real glory was in the 18th century. It then became a hugely fashionable spa, attracting English high society. In 1754 the architect John Wood the Elder began building the Circus at Bath that was finished after his death by his son John Wood the Younger. (This was a speculative housing development, of course, not an arena.) Wood's genius lay in treating the facades of a circle of separate if terraced houses as one giant building, giving them the same triple

▲ *The Circus in Bath echoes the Colosseum in form, name and even decoration – three tiers of windows flanked by the three orders of column – but not in its function.*

tiers of embedded columns – respectively Doric, Ionic and an unusual type of Corinthian – as the Colosseum. Unlike the amphitheatre, the Circus's facades face inwards across the square. The result is both majestic and convenient. Wood's innovation in turning terraced houses into what looks like one monumental building was in turn widely imitated, although more often as a half-circle or crescent than as a full circle.

it in one's mind. In memory we think it is smaller and then return to it again to find it every time greater than before.'

'Nobody who has never tried it can imagine the beauty of a walk through Rome by moonlight. Every detail is swallowed up by the great masses of light and shade, and only the grandest general outlines are visible. We have just enjoyed three of the brightest and most glorious nights – the Colosseum looks especially beautiful at this time. At night it is always closed. A hermit inhabits a small chapel and beggars of all sorts nestle beneath its crumbling arches. These men had built a fire on the level ground and a soft breeze had blown the smoke into the arena, so that the lower part of the ruins were hidden by it and only the huge masses of the building loomed out of the darkness before our eyes. As we stood at the railing and watched the scene, above our heads the moon shone brightly and calmly. Gradually the smoke filtered through holes and crannies and in the moonlight it seemed like fog. It was a marvellous sight.

Wolfgang von Goethe, *Italian Journey*, 2 February 1787

LORD BYRON

After the long disruption of the Napoleonic Wars (1793–1815), which had made travel around Europe very difficult, tourists began returning in increasing numbers. Now Rome was seen in an essentially Romantic light, especially by Byron, the most Romantic poet of all. Byron's retinue – a coach emblazoned with his coat of arms and accompanied by baggage horses and a shaggy Swiss mastiff – rode into the city on 29 April 1817. He decided to spend three weeks there seeing the sights. Nothing inspired him more than the Colosseum and he turned his impressions into poetry:

▲ Washerwomen in the Ruins of the Colosseum, *c1780, Robert Hubert. A French painter who spent 11 years in Rome as a young man, Hubert painted many proto-Romantic pictures of the city's monuments. (Alamy)*

I see before me the Gladiator lie:
He leans upon his hand - his manly brow
Consents to death, but conquers agony,
And his drooped head sinks gradually low –
And through his side the last drops, ebbing slow
From the red gash, fall heavy, one by one,
Like the first of a thunder-shower; and now
The arena swims around him – he is gone,
Ere ceased the inhuman shout which hailed the wretch who
  won…
But here, where Murder breathed her bloody steam;
And here where buzzing nations choked the ways,
And roared or murmured like a mountain stream
Dashing or dwindling as its torrent strays;
Here, where the Roman million's blame or praise
Was death or life, the playthings of a crowd,
My voice sounds much – and fall the stars' faint rays
On the arena void – seats crushed – walls bowed –
And galleries where my steps seem echoes faintly loud.
A ruin – yet what a ruin! From its mass
Walls, palaces, half-cities have been reared;
Yet oft the enormous skeleton you pass,
And marvel where the spoil could have appeared.
Hath it indeed been plundered, or but cleared?
Alas, developed, opens the decay,
When the colossal fabric's form is neared;

It will not bear the brightness of the day
Which streams too much on all years and man have reft away.
But when the rising moon begins to climb
Its topmost arch, and gently pauses there;
When the stars twinkle through the loops of time,
And the low night breeze waves along the air
The garland-forest which the grey walls wear,
Like laurels on the bald first Caesar's head;
When the light shines serene but does not glare,
Then in this magic circle raise the dead;
Heroes have trod this spot – 'tis on their dust ye tread.

Lord Byron, *Childe Harold's Pilgrimage* Canto 4, 1818

PERCY BYSSHE SHELLEY

Shelley, another poet and lover of Rome – he is buried there – took a less histrionic view but was equally impressed. Writing to his friend the novelist T.L. Peacock in November 1818, he remarked: 'The Coliseum is unlike any work of human hands I ever saw before. It is of enormous height and circuit, and the arches built of massive stones are piled on one another and jut into the blue air, shattered into the forms of overhanging rocks. It has been changed by time into an amphitheatre of rocky hills overgrown by the wild olive, the myrtle and the fig tree and threaded by little paths which wind among its ruined stairs and immeasurable galleries …' Clearly the Colosseum was still very much a ruin.

HENRY WADSWORTH LONGFELLOW

Visiting Europe on a youthful Grand Tour, Longfellow had a suitably poetic reaction to the amphitheatre in 1828. 'Silence, and the quiet moonbeams, and the broad deep shadows of the ruined wall… At length I came to an open space where the arches above had crumbled away, leaving the pavement an unroofed terrace high in the air. From this point, I could see the whole interior of the amphitheatre spread out beneath me, half in shadow, half in light, with such soft and indefinite outline that it seemed less an earthly reality than a reflection in the bosom of a lake … I did not conjure up the past, for the past had already become identified with the present.'

HENRY JAMES

Victorian visitors often liked to view the amphitheatre by moonlight, when it looked even more poetic. In *Daisy Miller* (1878), Henry James described a moonlit encounter in the arena, which proves fatal to his heroine, for Daisy succumbs to a 'Roman fever' and dies only a few days later. The time when tourists, literary or otherwise, could wander freely around the arena in romantic reverie was, however, coming to a close.

CHARLES DICKENS

By 1844 Charles Dickens was already immensely successful and famous as a novelist. He was also in need of a rest, so he took a break from novel writing to visit Italy, travelling with his family through the peninsula for nearly a year. Dickens visited the usual cities: Genoa, Naples, Florence, Rome and Venice, looking at contemporary life as much as the historical sites.

▲ The Colosseum *by Caspar van Wittel, from around1700. Born in Amsterdam, Wittel moved to Rome to paint picturesque but not always entirely accurate views. (Getty)*

It was probably Rome, and especially the Colosseum, that made the greatest impact on him. The result was *Pictures from Italy*, published in 1846. The book consists of a series of vivid snapshots of different parts of Italy, written with the usual Dickensian gusto especially when describing Italian street life:

It is no fiction but plain, sober honest Truth to say: so suggestive and distinct is it [the Colosseum] at this hour that for a moment – actually in passing in – they who will may have the whole great pile before them, as it used to be with thousands of eager faces staring down into the arena, and such a whirl of strife and blood and dust going on down there as no language can describe. Its solitude, its awful beauty and its utter desolation strike upon the stranger the next moment like a softened sorrow. And never in his life, perhaps, will he be so moved and overcome by any sight…

To see it crumbling there, an inch a year, its walls and arches overgrown with green, its corridors open to the day, the long grass growing in its porches, young trees of yesterday springing up on its ragged parapets and bearing fruit … To see its Pit of Fight filled up with earth, and the peaceful Cross planted in the centre … Never in its bloodiest prime can the sight of the gigantic Colosseum, full and running over with the lustiest life, have moved one heart as it must move all who look upon it now, a ruin. GOD be thanked, a ruin!

Charles Dickens, *Pictures from Italy*, 1846

THE MODERN ERA

The collapse of the French empire in 1814 had put further major excavations on hold for more than half a century. Only when Italy was finally united in 1870 and Rome became its new capital did archaeologists begin digging again in earnest. The office of the Superintendent of the Excavation and Preservation of the Monuments was established to encourage excavations in the Forum and the Colosseum. (It still exists.) Now that they had the wholehearted backing of the government, archaeologists moved swiftly to rid the amphitheatre of most of its Christian trappings – the new Italy was determinedly secular – and to demolish the buildings that had long grown up around and inside the amphitheatre. Nothing was to detract from the naked majesty of the arena.

Digging began in 1874 at the eastern end of the arena and soon uncovered the herringbone brick floor (*opus spicatum*) and the entrance to the main axial drain. In 1876 John Henry Parker of the Ashmolean Museum in Oxford published a book, *The Archaeology of Rome: The Colosseum* about the diggings. This contained highly important photographs and drawings of parts of the Colosseum that have since been lost, but Parker himself had some very unsound views. He thought that much of the amphitheatre had been built under Nero (*ie* before AD68) and that some of the surrounding tufa walls were even older.

The archaeologists of the 1870s, by digging far deeper than any earlier excavators had, revealed the full depth of the subterranean structure of the *hypogeum*. Unfortunately, they had not reckoned on the problem of flooding that the shape of the *cavea* encouraged. Their diggings soon flooded with

water, which turned stagnant and repellent. Only in 1879 were these waters drained. By then over half the arena's floor had been removed, rendering further tourists' moonlit rambles almost impossible. (The remaining section of the floor survived intact until the 1930s.)

THE FASCIST INTERLUDE

In 1922 Mussolini made himself dictator of Italy in a coup d'état, taking the title Duce, from the Latin dux, leader. He soon began to talk of creating a new Roman Empire that would rival if not surpass the original, and he started to call the Mediterranean 'Mare Nostrum', our sea, as the an-cient Romans had done. Five maps were put up on a wall of the Basilica of Maxentius in the Fo-rum Romanum showing the expansion of Rome's empire from its modest beginnings to its most expansive under Trajan in AD116.

◄ This rare 19th-century photograph allows us to see the interior of the Colosseum interior just before the 1874 excavations were begun. The photograph was taken in 1867 and the cross in the centre that was removed is clearly visible, as are grave stones and mausoleums that encircle it. (Alamy)

▲ Mussolini (centre) rides his troops past the Colosseum after the opening of Via dei Fori Imperiali, in October 1932, a new wide road to encircle the city's ancient monuments. (Getty)

The last of these maps – which has since been removed – displayed Mussolini's vision for a new 'Roman empire'. This was to have included Albania, the coast of Croatia, many of the Greek islands, Corsica and Nice taken from France, and much of Africa from Tunisia east to Libya and Egypt and then down through the Sudan to Ethiopia and Somalia. By 1942 some of these areas were in fact occupied by Italian troops, but they never began to form part of a stable, unified em-pire.

Mussolini's grandiose ideas involved, among other things, trying to give 20th-century Rome broad imperial avenues to rival those of Paris, Vienna or Berlin. As no streets so wide and straight had ever existed in Rome before, even under the emperors, Mussolini decided to drive brand new boulevards through the ancient city.

The driving of the Via dei Fori Imperiali (Street of the Imperial Forums) in the 1930s straight through the very centre of Rome involved the demolition of many historic buildings, not just those from the medieval, Renaissance and Baroque eras but even of some monuments that had survived from antiquity. Mussolini himself was photographed wielding a pick to demolish old buildings whose picturesque but untidy appearance did not suit his ideas of virile neo-Romanism. But the damage he instigated was not restricted just to medieval and Renaissance buildings.

The top of the Meta Sudens, the fountain to the north of the Colosseum, was removed and the base of the statue of the colossal Helios statue destroyed, after both had survived

millennia of neglect and depredation. Down by the Tiber the Ara Augusta Pacis, the altar of the Augustan peace erected by the emperor Augustus in 13BC to celebrate the return of lasting peace to the Roman world, was dug up in 1938, moved to near the Mausoleum of Augustus and hastily and inaccurate-ly reconstructed. A large pavilion was built around it by Vittorio Morpurgo, a Rationalist or neo-classical architect, who worked in the style favoured by the regime. (While willing to work for the Fascist regime, Morpurgo happened to be Jewish – plenty of Italian Jews had joined the Fascist Party earlier in the 1920s. His Jewishness meant that he was unable to enter his own creation after the adoption of new anti-Semitic laws in Italy in late 1938, a hideous irony. Happily, Morpurgo survived the Second World War.)

Mussolini also ordered the razing of the maze of small streets around the Campo dei Fiori to reveal the temples of the Largo Argentina, the ancient site of Pompey's Theatre. And he knocked down the old buildings that surrounded the Pantheon and the Columns of Trajan and Marcus Au-relius. These wholesale demolitions and reconstructions were part of Mussolini's vision to turn the city into a mixture of ancient Roman theme park and bombastic neo-imperial capital. His aim, how-ever, was less to display and explore the past than

▲ *Hitler being shown around the interior of the Colosseum in May 1938 by Giuseppe Bottai, the Fascist Education Minister, here shown on Hitler's left. No ancient building in Rome delighted Hitler more than the Colosseum did. (Alamy)*

to glorify the new Fascist state, trampling over local rights where necessary. Such thoughtless damage even to ancient Roman monuments was typical of the brutal blindness of il Duce's programme. Historic Rome suffered more from Fascist 'renovation' than it had from any of its numerous sacks.

The Colosseum itself was not directly damaged but, in being turned into a stadium for Fascist political rallies, it suffered inappropriate and clumsy alterations. Unsuitable stairs were built between the first and second levels and asphalt floors were laid to permit the crowds of jackbooted Fascists to move around the arena more freely.

The building of the first line of Rome's Metro, the city's underground/subway network, in 1939 led to the digging of a trench very close to the amphitheatre. The trench almost touched the building's foundations and caused a further round of flooding in the basement. However, Giuseppe Cozzo, an Italian engineer, was able to excavate the western end of the arena systemati-cally in 1937–1939. Cozzo had been studying the basement for years, so he was able to correct many of Parker's errors. He also discovered the location of Ludus Magnus, the main training school for gladiators nearby, although it was not to be fully excavated until the 1950s.

HITLER'S VISIT TO ROME

In May 1938 Hitler paid a visit to Italy to cement his still relatively new alliance with Mussolini and, perhaps more importantly for him, to see the buildings and ruins that he had so long admired. After stopping off in Florence, where he enthused over the more monumental aspects of the Renaissance, the Führer arrived in Rome with an entourage of some 500 Nazi officials, including Goebbels and Ribbentrop. A special station, the Ostiense, was built for the distinguished German visitors' trains. There Mussolini and King Victor Emmanuel II waited to greet the Führer. Swastikas flew over the city and a new street was named in Hitler's honour, Via Adolf Hitler. (It has since been renamed.)

Over the next two days, between official engagements, Hitler spent hours touring ancient Rome's monuments. He was particularly impressed by the Colosseum, seeing it as the supreme example of Roman imperial engineering at its most grandiose. (The Pantheon was the other building that most excited him and he spent hours alone beneath its dome, lost in dreams of imperial grandeur.) Mussolini, who did not share his guest's burning enthusiasm for ancient architecture, soon made his excuses, so Hitler was guided around the Colosseum by the Education Minister Giuseppi Bottai. Although he was a hard line Fascist and a keen proponent of Italy's new German alliance and consequent new anti-Semitic laws, Bottai reportedly did not find Hitler easy company. The effect of seeing such monuments at first hand filled Hitler with a passion to replicate the amphitheatre's and the temple's majesty but on a vastly larger scale in his megalomaniac schemes for rebuilding Berlin. He positively relished the ruinous state of the amphitheatre, as it fitted his ideals of Ruinenwerttheorie, pioneered by his favourite architect Albert Speer: that great buildings should look even more imposing in a state of ruin than they did when intact, impressing generations to come.

The Fascist regime in Italy collapsed in 1943. In the bitter fighting that followed, as the Allied armies slowly pushed the German Army out of Italy, Rome itself escaped relatively lightly. Although at one point in 1944 German troops reportedly sheltered under the very arches of the amphitheatre, the building itself was never bombed, shelled or requisitioned. (Rome was in fact declared a *città aperta*, an open city, sparing it from the bitter fighting that wrecked so many of Europe's cities.)

THE POST-WAR ERA

After 1945, the Colosseum turned into a circus in a new and undesirable sense. The growth in prosperity during Italy's post-war economic miracle led to increasing traffic across the city. The amphitheatre itself became a roundabout, with cars coming from Mussolini's new Via dei Fori Imperiali streaming endlessly around it. Crossing the street to enter the Colosseum meant taking your life in your hands. Meanwhile further archaeological investigation slowed to a crawl.

Happily in the 1980s Rome's City Council rerouted the traffic, so making the whole area around the Forum traffic free and reasonably peaceful. Repairs on the actual structure restarted, with part of the arena floor area being restored by 2000, once more giving the *hypogeum* beneath it some protection from the weather.

SQUARE COLOSSEUM

One of the most curious creations of the Fascist years is the Palazzo della Civiltà Italiana, the Museum of Italian Civilisation, popularly known as the Colosseo Quadrato, the Square Colosseum. It is in fact Mussolini's tribute to the great amphitheatre and is located in the EUR complex south of the city that he commissioned.

The initials stand for Esposizione Universale Roma, Rome World Fair. Begun in 1936, the site was meant to host the World Fair of 1942. Not by coincidence, this would have marked the 20th anniversary of the founding of the Fascist state. The outbreak of the Second World War doomed this plan, however, and work on the site was finally abandoned in 1941. After the war the buildings, many of which are fine examples of the Rationalist style, combining neoclassical elements such as columns and arches with sleek modern lines, were completed, and EUR became a business centre.

The Colosseo Quadrato is the most remarkable building in the complex and one of the most appealing of the whole era. It is not overpoweringly large unlike many Fascist buildings. Designed in 1937 to host the Mostra della Civiltà Romana (Exhibition of Roman Civilisation) by the architects Giovanni Guerrini, Ernesto Bruno La Padula and Mario Romano, it was inaugurated on 30 November 1940.

The palazzo has six tiers of nine arches, surpassing the original Colosseum's four stories. Each of the arches was originally intended to have a neoclassical statue in it, as the Colosseum once had, representing heroes or gods. Along the podium on which the palazzo is built there still stand 28 statues, personifications of various virtues or sciences such as astronomy, medicine, agriculture and mathematics, while at each corner of the podium are equestrian statues, two of them representing the Dioscuri, the original 'Heavenly Twins'. (Some observers have noted the palazzo's strange, presumably unintended resemblance to buildings in Giorgio de Chirico's metaphysical paintings, created 20 years before.)

The palazzo is built of polished white travertine stone that looks very like marble and still gleams whitely, seeming almost pristine. At times since its construction the Square Colosseum, which is not perhaps the most practical of buildings, has been empty but since 2015 it has been the headquarters of the luxury fashion label Fendi, that makes silk and leather goods. The ground floor of the building has been left free to house temporary exhibitions of Italian craftsmanship.

7

THE COLOSSEUM TODAY

VISITING THE COLOSSEUM

By the late 20th century the Colosseum, like so many ancient monuments, had become a victim of its own fame. Overrun by huge numbers of tourists, begrimed by centuries of pollution – much of it coming from 20th-century road traffic – its majestic if half-ruined exterior concealed a bewildering jumble of wrecked stones and rubble. There was hardly any surface left on which to walk around and admire the interior, thanks to nearly two centuries of archaeological investigations that have ploughed up the earthen floor. The more fastidious visitors to Rome were starting to give the landmark a complete miss.

Happily, a new millennium brought new initiatives. A €25 million (c£20 million/$30 million) restoration programme funded by Tod's, the luxury shoe and bag maker, began in 2013 and was triumphantly concluded in 2016. This has cleaned up and restored the arena's facade so that the travertine stone once more glows a gentle creamy-gold. The toilet and lift facilities have been improved, a visitors' centre with a cafe is promised and the stairways have been made less daunting, although they remain notably steep. The prime minister of Italy, Matteo Renzi, attended the official reopening of the restored amphitheatre in July 2016. (In fact it had never really closed, tourism at the Colosseum being too important to interrupt.)

A further €18 million (c£16 million/$21 million) is now being spent on making the arena floor more usable for contemporary entertainments. The Colosseum, however, is unlikely to rival the arenas of Verona or Arles, or even the Baths of Caracalla in Rome, as a venue for music or theatre in the near future, despite Paul McCartney having played there to a select audience of just 400 in 2003. No one wants to cover over the whole *hypogeum* again while the great majority of seating places in the *cavea* remain ruined so are completely unusable.

Now that the area around the Colosseum and the adjacent Forum Romanum looks set to remain traffic free – much to the annoyance of some local shopkeepers – the Colosseum can hope to keep its new clean look. A lot remains to be done, most of it in important if unglamorous areas such as drainage. Some of the drains currently in use go back to Roman times. As in imperial times, the repairs and upkeep of the great structure are once more an ongoing task.

A SYMBOL OF LIFE AND MERCY

The Colosseum, site of so much bloodshed and brutality in the distant past, found a different role recently as a beacon of human clemency, taking as its slogan 'The Colosseum lights up life'. A campaign in 1999, which won the support of Amnesty International, lit up the amphitheatre's exterior in a golden light each night that a death sentence was commuted anywhere in the world, or when any country votes to abolish or suspend capital punishment. As the Egyptian news agency Al-Ahram put it, 'this noxious landmark… this ancient killing ground has become a symbol of life and mercy.'

All this restoration has made the difficulties of visiting the great amphitheatre without being mobbed even more acute. The number of visitors per year is now thought to be heading past the 6 million mark. Although the Colosseum in its prime could accommodate around 50,000 spectators at a single sitting, those audiences were well disciplined. Ancient Romans sat down and stayed in their allotted places once they had entered. Modern visitors, by contrast, don't. This is partly because they are restricted in practice to just two levels of seats.

▶ *Despite less than half of the original building surviving into this century, the Colosseum is among the most imposing buildings in Rome. Now with its hypogeum partially restored, it is today far more accessible.*

▼ *An advantage of the ruinous state of the Colosseum is that it allows visitors a view of the bones of the huge structure.*

▶ *The exterior of the northeast of the Colosseum covered in scaffolding during the latest series of restoration works, photographed in October 2014.*

THE BEST TIMES AND WAYS TO VISIT

The Colosseum is open every day from 8.30am to one hour before sunset. Crowds queuing up for admittance can form a long, thick line curling round the arena at almost any time of day and, perhaps more surprisingly, at almost any time of year. Going early on a rainy morning in November does not guarantee swift entry, let alone any peace once inside to muse upon past glories. Planning ahead is essential. (If you are part of an organised group, obviously your guide will arrange such matters.)

To obtain a ticket on the day it is better to buy one at the Palatine Museum, about five minutes' walk away, than at the Colosseum itself. This ticket also gives entry to the Palatine Museum, itself very much worth a visit. Better still, however, is to buy a Roma Pass online. A Roma Pass gives free entry to one or two museums (depending on the exact type chosen), half-price entry to most other museums – though not to the Vatican, for it is a separate state – and free travel on Rome's rather skeletal bus, metro and tram systems for the two or three days the pass lasts. There is a metro stop right opposite the amphitheatre. With a Roma Pass you simply go to the

queue for groups, which is usually much shorter than that for individual ticket holders. If you feel like it, you can pose for photographs just outside the arena with modern 'gladiators', professional re-enactors costumed plausibly enough.

While going early in the morning in the autumn or winter may not avoid the crowds, going at lunchtime, around 1pm, can sometimes thin them out. Tour groups like their lunch. The disadvantage, at least in summer, is that the *cavea,* now without any *velarium* to shade it, can grow infernally hot. Take a hat and plenty of water with you. (Or conversely, if it looks

▼ ▶ *The interior of the Colosseum looking in far better condition in July 2016 after a massive clean-up. The corridors are also now more accessible to visitors. (Getty, below)*

▲ *An aerial view of the Colosseum with the Alban Hills clearly visible in the background. The scaffolding surrounding most of the extant facade has since come down, and the great bulk of the Flavian Amphitheatre once more dominates the city.*

cloudy, take an umbrella for any downpours.) There are varied touts and stalls just outside the arena selling water, ice cream and snacks but they can be absurdly expensive, it is best to take your own food and drinks with you into the arena; just as many Romans did during the time of the Empire.

▲ *The head of Tod, the luxury shoe maker, Diego Della Valle (right) with Gianni Alemanno, then mayor of Rome, discuss the 25 million euro restoration programme in January 2011. This began in 2013 and was finished in 2016. (Getty)*

▼ *The exterior of the Colosseum at night after the recent restoration, which has ensured that its majestic triple tiers of arched openings still rise above the Forum Romanum. The way it is illuminated at night gives some idea of how it must have looked centuries ago.*

INSIDE THE COLOSSEUM

It can be a good idea to walk around the exterior of the Colosseum before entering to try to get your bearings. Doing so will reveal that more than half the exterior wall has vanished. It is also easy to spot the very obvious restoration works that have taken place over the centuries. The external entrance for visitors does not at all coincide with where you emerge into the *cavea*. One way of keeping your bearings is to look towards where the main outer wall is preserved and remember that this extant section is on the *north* side of the arena.

Once inside you are directed through some very atmospheric passageways to one of the two levels open to tourists, one on the ground floor and one on the first floor, which is actually less than halfway up. The other levels are closed and you cannot always walk all the way round even those that are open due to the continuing restoration works. If you are not feeling like a steep climb on a hot day, you should take one of the lifts up to the first floor.

When you emerge blinking in the sunlight, as ancient spectators must have once done, you get a fine view of the whole building, including the arena floor and much of the *hypogeum*. Most of this is now fully exposed but is not currently open to the general public. Behind, inside the passageways on this floor and the ones below, small displays of archaeological or architectural fragments such as capitals or carvings are arranged in no obvious order. These reveal most strikingly how the Colosseum was in a constant state of repair and alteration throughout the imperial centuries. There are also some small displays of contemporary art.

The ground floor tempts you by offering a chance to walk on the wooden floor that has been built as a partial reconstruction of the original arena floor, which was built under Domitian. Frustratingly, parts of this are also often closed off. But it is possible to see certain things close-up, such as the remains of some of the stucco decoration that would once have covered most interior surfaces in the vault of one of the main passages just to the left of the central entrance way.

THE HYPOGEUM

Although you may normally shun all forms of organised tour, one area of the Colosseum is still closed to individual visitors: the *hypogeum*, the two-storied underworld once central to the functioning of the arena. This has been much restored recently, although work is ongoing, parts of the *hypogeum* being closed off unpredictably. At the time of writing the whole underground area is not accessible. Enough of the labyrinth, however, has been restored to give a far better impression of how it must have looked during the imperial centuries than previously.

To visit the *hypogeum* at present you have to go with an organised group, unless you are an accredited academic or VIP. Tours are not included in the general tickets nor does the Roma Pass let you join one but have to be purchased separately. At present the tours in English leave at 9.20, 9.40, 10.40, 11.20, 11.40, 12.20, 13.20 and 16.20. They take about 20–25 minutes. Tickets currently cost 30 euros (about £28/$36) – there are some concessions – and can be bought

▼ *Aerial views can give a better idea of the amphitheatre in its totality than walking around or inside it. Here it is apparent that less than half of the original facade wall has survived the depredations of quarrying thieves down the centuries.*

▼ *During the Middle Ages parts of the Colosseum, which had become home to Romans who defended their property rights there, were used to grow vegetables. It still offers surprisingly good growing conditions, as these plants reveal.*

▲ *The partly reconstructed wooden floor that now covers part of the* hypogeum, *with behind it the small section of seating that was restored in the 1930s. Probably knights (members of the Equestrian Order) originally occupied these seats.*

▼ *Part of the recently restored and now reopened* hypogeum, *photographed in September 2013 during the Colosseum's latest reconstruction programme.*

on site or in advance at one of several websites. For those really interested in the workings of the amphitheatre, the cost is well worth it, for a knowledgeable guide is essential to appreciating the *hypogeum*. For example, they will point out the small markings recently made on the walls to indicate where lifts were, a point that can easily be overlooked by the non-expert.

Although all accessible parts of the Colosseum are nowadays usually thronged with visitors – except sometimes at lunch – the overall effect of seeing the huge arena inside and out is still powerfully moving, and gives a vivid impression of ancient Rome.

▼ *The upper part of one of the immense brick, cement and stone buttresses that make up the skeleton of the Colosseum.*

GLOSSARY

Acclamatio	Applause or shouts of disapproval from amphitheatre audience
Ambulacra	Outer passageways of the Colosseum
Amphitheatre	Literally 'double theatre', the Colosseum being the greatest example
Annona	Wheat ration doled out to poorer Roman citizens
Architrave	Stone or marble beam or lintel
Arcuated	Architecture reliant on vaults and arches, as Roman architecture was
Auctorati	Free men, often bankrupts, who volunteered as gladiators
Bestiarii	Men who fought animals
Capital	Head or crowning feature of a column
Cavea	Seating area of a theatre or amphitheatre
Cena libera	Free dinner given in public to gladiators the night before the fight
Circus	Stadium used for chariot races and also for gladiatorial games and public executions. In Rome the Circus Maximus was much the biggest
Collegium	Guild or association to which most ordinary Roman citizens belonged
Corinthian	Third, most elaborate of the three classical orders of column
Crucifixion	The normal method of execution for serious crimes favoured by the Romans; reputedly Carthaginian in origin
Cuneus	Literally 'wedge'. Wedge-shaped areas of seating in the Colosseum
Damnati	Criminals condemned to death, often in the Colosseum
Damnatio ad bestias	Criminals condemned to death by being attacked by wild animals
Doctores	Men, normally retired gladiators, who taught trainee gladiators
Domus aurea	Literally 'golden house', Nero's immense palace that was partly demolished after his fall in AD68 and on whose site the Colosseum was built
Doric	First and simplest of the classical orders of columns. In Roman buildings, normally smooth and with a base; in Greek architecture fluted (corrugated) and without a base
Editor	The person who put on and usually paid for the games
Eques/equites	Literally horsemen: mounted gladiators who usually started the main show by riding around the arena before dismounting to fight

Essedaria	Chariot-driving gladiators, at times female, often coming from Britain
Familia	Group or 'family' of gladiators in a *ludus*, training school
Fascia	Band of protective leather around a gladiator's legs and thighs
Galerus	Long steel shoulder-guard worn by a *retiarius*
Gaul	Area of northwest Europe inhabited mostly by Celts and conquered by Julius Caesar; today France, Belgium, western Switzerland, south Holland and west bank of the Rhine
Gladius	Short Roman stabbing sword, the main weapon of many gladiators and of all legionaries
Harenari	Attendants who refreshed the arena's bloodied sand between gladiatorial acts
Honestiores	Upper class of Roman citizen with superior legal rights, a distinction that emerged under Hadrian AD117–138
Hoplomachus	Heavily armed gladiator with helmet and small round shield, derived from Greek soldiers called *hoplites*
Hypogeum	Underground sections of Colosseum, that housed the scenery and wild animals
Ima cavea	The lowest or best section of the *cavea* proper
Inamoratae	Women who had fallen desperately in love with gladiators
Infamis	Someone without any rights or social status, outcast. Gladiators were classified as *infames*
Inferiores	Lower class of Roman citizen, a distinction that emerged from the 2nd century AD on
Insulae	Apartment blocks, home to most Roman citizens, often flimsily built and prone to burning down
Ionic	Second of the classical orders of columns, with voluted capitals
Lanista	Trainer of gladiators who often also purchased and rented them out
Ludus	Training school for gladiators (also game, sport)
Maenianum	Seating level in the auditorium. The Colosseum had four levels
Manica	Leather and metal arm-guard mostly worn by a retiarius
Manubiae	Money from sale of war loot
Medicus	Doctors who looked after gladiators. Galen was the most famous

Media cavea	The 19 rows of marble benches in the mid-section of the *cavea* seating the middle classes of Rome: citizens able to afford a proper toga. Also called *maenianum secundum* or second balcony
Meridianum spectaculum	The noonday spectacle of public executions, often avoided by upper-class Romans who deplored the lack of skills involved
Missio	Release, mercy, often granted defeated gladiators who had fought well. The decision was down to the *editor* concerned, who in the Colosseum was usually the emperor
Munus/munera	Gladiatorial game(s); originally offerings or tributes to the gods at funerals. Hence the link between gladiatorial games
Murmillo	Heavily armoured gladiator with a metal fish on his helmet
Naumachia	Mock sea battles
Naumacharii	Combatants forced to man the ships in a *naumachia*. Unlike proper gladiators, they were untrained and most were killed in each event
Opus caementicum	Roman concrete, which made amphitheatres and similar huge arcuated structures possible
Opus signinum	Waterproof concrete used in aqueducts and perhaps in parts of the *hypogeum*
Parmula	Small round shield
Parmularii	Gladiators such as Thracians armed with small round shields
Pegniarii	Play-gladiators who fought with wooden swords before the main act, usually without fatalities
Pilaster	Rectangular decorative column sunk into wall and playing no structural role
Podium	In the Colosseum: row of seats closest to the arena reserved for senators and other VIPs, such as the Vestal Virgins or ambassadors
Pollice verso	Literally, 'turned thumb', sign indicating life or death for defeated gladiators. Probably thumbs were turned up and in for death, down and out for release
Pompa	Grand procession of the gladiators at the start of the games
Primus palus	Literally, 'first stake': the top grade of gladiator
Provocator	Literally 'challenger', heavily armoured gladiator with a distinctive breast plate
Pyrriarchi	Condemned criminals who were burnt alive
Quadriga	Four-horse chariot statue; one stood above the main entrance to the Colosseum

Retiarius	Lightly armed, agile gladiator who fought with net and trident often paired off with *secutor*
Rudis	Wooden sword used by trainee gladiators; also given to victorious gladiators on retirement
Samnites	Early type of gladiator, originating probably in Campania
Scutum	Large shield used by legionaries and some gladiators
Secutor	Literally, 'pursuer'. Gladiator armed with large shield and sword who often fought the *retiarius*
Senate	Supreme political body of Rome, composed mainly of ex-magistrates
Spectacula	Performances, especially by gladiators
Spina	Literally, 'spine': the central barrier in the Circus Maximus
Spoliarum	Place where gladiators' corpses were stripped of their armour
Subligaculum	Loincloth worn by most gladiators
Subsellium	Bench or seat in the amphitheatre and elsewhere
Summa cavea	Highest tier of seats reserved for non-citizens
Summum maenianum in ligneis	Topmost circle of the *cavea* mostly built of wood with standing room only for slaves and freedmen
Thracian	Also known as Thraex, a gladiator from Thrace, like Spartacus, who fought with small shield
Tiro	Novice gladiator who had fought in a contest and survived
Travertine	Hard white limestone used in main parts of Colosseum
Tuba	Roman war trumpet used in arena orchestras
Tufa	Soft brown volcanic stone used in less visible parts of Colosseum
Tuscan	Shortest and thickest type of column, Italian in origin
Unctores	Masseurs employed in the Ludus to keep gladiators fit
Velarium	Awning spread over the *cavea* of amphitheatres
Venatio/nes	Wild animal 'hunt/s' in the arena
Venatores	Wild animal hunters
Veteranus	Literally, 'veteran', an experienced gladiator
Virtus	Roman quality meaning courage, manliness, integrity, ability
Volute	Spiral scroll at each end of an Ionic column, based possibly on a ram's horn
Vomitorium	Arch allowing rapid entry/exit of spectators into the *cavea*
Voussoir	Wedge-shaped stone or brick block in arch

INDEX

acoustics 52
Aemilius Lepidus 67
Alaric 31
Alberti, Leon Battista 132
Alexander Severus, emperor 28
amphitheatres
  architectural form 36
  history and development 36–47
  wooden 18, 20, 22, 36, 57, 66
  see also Colosseum
Androcles and the Lion 75
animals *see* wild beast shows
  (*venationes*)
Annibaldi family 129
Anthony, Mark 101
Antoninus Pius, emperor 26
Appian 98
Apuleius 78
Ara Augusta Pacis 141
arcades (*fornices*) 28
Arch of Constantine 120
Arch of Titus 24, 25
arched entrances (*vomitoria*) 9, 52, 53,
  54–5, 109, 113
Arles amphitheatre 27, 52
Arval Brethren 112
Astrodome, Houston 11
auditorium (*cavea*) 9, 37, 52, 115
  see also seating
Augustine, St 120, 121
Augustus, emperor 27, 29, 37, 52, 57,
  67, 73, 75, 80, 97, 111, 113, 115
Aulus Gellius 75
Aurelian, emperor 29
awning (*velarium*) 6, 24, 39, 46, 52, 54,
  59–60, 110

Battle of the Milvian Bridge
  (AD312) 30
bears 70, 73
Bede, Venerable 32, 127
Benedict XIV, Pope 8, 76, 134
birds 73
Bottai, Giuseppe 142
Bruegel, Peter (the Elder) 132, 133
bulls, bullfights 73, 129–30
burning alive, death by (*pyrriarchi*) 75,
  76
Byron, Lord 32, 138–9
Byzantine Empire 29

Caerleon amphitheatre 27
Caesar, Julius 20, 57, 67, 69, 87
Caesarea 47
Caligula, emperor 20, 27, 80, 81, 93,
  101, 102
Capua amphitheatre 87
Carrara marble 52
Carthage 25, 77
Cassiodorus 124–6
Cassius Dio 26, 28, 57–8, 73, 103
Cellini, Benvenuto 131
cement 58
chariots
  quadriga 45, 48, 54, 61, 72, 112, 113
  races 64, 96, 108
Charlemagne, emperor 127
Chester amphitheatre 27
Christians, Christianity 29, 30, 74,
  120–1, 124
  martyrs 6, 8, 30, 44–5, 75, 76–7, 134
  papacy 128, 129, 130
Cicero 67, 93, 94, 101, 118
Circus, Bath 137
Circus Maximus 18–19, 27, 28, 64, 70,
  75, 76, 108
civil wars 18, 27, 29, 67, 101
Claudius, emperor 43, 44, 57, 69, 74, 96
Clement X, Pope 134
Clement XI, Pope 134
Coliseum, London 11, 32
Colosseo Quadrato (Square
  Colosseum) 143
Colosseum
  acoustics 52
  archetypal emblem of Rome 6, 27,
    127, 130, 132
  artistic and cultural influences 132–3,
    136, 136–9, 137, 140, 143
  Christian shrines and ceremonies 76,
    134, 135
  conveniences and amenities 118
  design and construction 9, 48–61
  dimensions 24, 60
  excavation 134, 140, 141–2
  flora 129
  inauguration 23, 32, 57, 100
  looted and quarried 8, 126, 128, 130–1
  models of 108, 134–5
  modern era 140–3
  name variants 32

repurposed 129, 134
restoration and conservation 134,
  140, 143, 146
seating capacity 6, 106
siting of 22, 23
structural damage and decay 8–9,
  28, 32, 125, 127, 128–9, 130
timeline 12–15
visiting 146–51
Colossus of Rhodes 21
columns 40, 52
  Composite 40
  Corinthian 37, 40, 50, 52, 137
  Doric 37, 40, 50, 52, 137
  Ionic 37, 40, 50, 52, 137
  Tuscan 40, 43
Commodus, emperor 27, 69, 81, 91,
  96, 102–3, 120
concrete (*opus caementicium*) 37, 42,
  47, 49
condemned men (*damnati*) 30, 51, 57,
  69, 74–5, 77, 81, 93
Constans II, emperor 126
Constantine I, emperor 29, 30, 74,
  87, 120
Constantinople (Istanbul) 29, 30, 124
Constantius II, emperor 6, 31
construction 48–61
  decoration 6, 25, 52, 53
  drainage system 48–9
  exterior walls 52
  foundations 49
  hypogeum 52
  labour force 51
  materials 47, 49–50, 52
  mechanical devices 61
  methods 60–1
  over-engineering 9, 128
  seating 51–2
corbels 46
Cozzo, Giuseppe 141–2
criminals
  condemned men (*damnati*) 30, 51,
    57, 69, 74–5, 77, 81, 93
  damnatio ad ludum gladiatorum 84
Curio, Caius Scribonius 22
Cyprian, St 90

Dacian Wars 26, 86, 87, 89, 106
Deva Victrix (Chester) amphitheatre 68

Dickens, Charles 139
Diocletian, emperor 29, 30
Domitian, emperor 24, 25, 48, 58, 80, 86, 88, 94, 98, 114, 115, 118
Domus Aurea (Golden Palace) 20, 21, 22, 46, 50
drainage systems 44, 48–9, 146

earthquakes 29, 32, 125, 127, 130, 134
Edict of Milan (AD313) 30
editor 27, 67, 68, 69, 78, 79, 81, 90, 91
El Djem amphitheatre 27, 113
elephants 57, 70, 73
emperor-worship 74
Epictetus 91
Epidaurus amphitheatre 38, 52
Etruscans 36, 67
Eugenius IV, Pope 132

Fascist era 140–3
Flavian Amphitheatre *see* Colosseum
flooding 23, 25, 52, 58, 59, 140, 141
Forum Boarium 66
Forum Romanum 18, 27, 36, 67, 126, 140, 146
Frangipani family 129
funerary games 66, 67, 100, 118

Galen 90, 91
Gallienus, emperor 120
Gérôme, Jean-Léon 19, 76, 77, 80, 81
Gibbon, Edward 103, 136
Gladiator (film) 78, 80, 102
gladiator schools 86–91
gladiatorial games (*munera*) 6, 8, 18, 23, 26–7, 28, 29, 30, 31, 36, 64–81
 advertising 68, 80
 banning of 8, 31
 decline in popularity 121
 disposal of the dead 81, 85
 earliest recorded 66
 final games 31, 124
 frequency 106
 gladiatorial combats 78–81
 morning hunt *see* wild beast shows (*venationes*)
 noonday spectacle (*meridianum spectaculum*) 74–7
 opening ceremonies 69
 organisation and programme 68–81
 origins 64–7
 political purposes 27, 64, 67, 120
 public executions 74–7, 77, 118
 re-enactments 92, 107
 scale of slaughter 6
 warm-up acts 78–9

gladiators 84–103
 accommodation and diet 68, 91
 aristocratic 84, 98, 100
 armour and weapons 69, 79, 87, 92, 93, 94, 95, 96
 bestiarius 70
 betting on 68
 equites 79, 93, 95–6, 101
 essedarii 96
 female 27, 97–8
 female admirers 84, 98, 117
 financial rewards 81
 glamour 84, 100, 117
 grades 91
 hoplomachus 69, 78, 93, 95
 imperial 102–3
 medical care 91
 military service 41, 66, 101
 murmillo 89, 93–4, 95, 96, 101
 names 98
 novices (*tiros*) 79, 90–1
 oath and contracts 89, 90
 play-gladiators (*pegniarii*) 74
 provocator 93, 94–5
 recruitment 84, 85
 retiarius 66, 67, 79, 80, 89, 90, 92, 94, 95, 97
 retirement 81, 90
 secutor 66, 67, 79, 90, 93, 94, 95, 97, 103
 social and political status 84–5
 theatrical skills 42
 Thracian/*Thraex* 69, 78, 90, 91, 93, 94, 95
 training 86–91
 venator 70, 86, 87, 89, 96
 veterans 69, 91, 100
 volunteers (*auctoratii*) 85, 91, 100, 101
 war captives 87, 88, 89, 93
 wounded gladiators 81, 90, 91
Goethe, Wolfgang von 136, 138
grain ration 51
Grand Tour 136–9
Great Fire (AD64) 20, 75
Great Persecution (AD306–310) 30
Greek theatres 37, 38
Gregory VII, Pope 129
Guiscard, Robert 129

Hadrian, emperor 26, 88
Hagia Sofia 124
'Hail Caesar: Those about to die salute you!' 69
Halicarnassus 97
Haterii family tomb 61
Herculaneum 53

Herod Agrippa II 113
Hitler, Adolf 142
Holy Roman Empire 127, 129
Honorius, emperor 31
Horace 86, 100
horsemen 79, 95–6
Hubert, Robert 138
hypogeum 6, 9, 25, 28, 36, 46, 48, 52, 55, 56–7, 64, 84, 150–1

Ignatius, St 76, 77
imperial box (*pulvinar*) 55, 69, 112

James, Henry 139
Jewish revolt (AD66) 22, 24, 25
Josephus 25, 74
Justinian, emperor 125
Juvenal 66, 80, 96, 117

knights 111, 115, 118

legionaries 41–2, 92
leopards 70, 72, 73
life and death decisions *see* mercy (*missio*)
lift system 56–7, 116
lightning strikes 28, 117
lions 57, 70, 73, 74, 75
Livy 100
Longfellow, Henry Wadsworth 139
Louis IV of Bavaria 129, 130
Lucangeli, Carlo 134
Ludus Dacicus 86, 89
Ludus Gallicus 86, 89
Ludus Magnus 69, 81, 85, 86, 88, 117, 142
Ludus Matutinus 70, 86, 89, 96

McCartney, Paul 146
marble 50, 52, 128, 130
Marcus Aurelius, emperor 26, 27, 91, 101, 102, 120
Martial 23, 32, 46, 48, 57, 73, 79, 85, 94, 98, 100
Maximus Magnus, emperor 87
mercy (*missio*) 79, 80, 81, 90, 100
Merida amphitheatre 89
Meta Sudans 24, 141
mining 30, 51, 88
Morpurgo, Vittorio 141
music 69, 79
Mussolini, Benito 140, 141, 142

Napoleon Bonaparte 134
naval battles, mock (*naumachia*) 23, 25, 52, 53, 56, 57–9, 64, 67, 69
necromancy 131

Nero, emperor 20, 22, 27, 57, 75, 76, 77, 84, 94, 98, 102, 118
Niessen, Wilhelm 140
Nîmes amphitheatre 64
noonday spectacle (*meridianum spectaculum*) 74–7
Normans 129

Odoacer 124
opening ceremony (*pompa*) 69
Orange 52
Ostrogoths 124, 125, 126
Otto III, emperor 127
Ovid 110, 111

Palatine Hill 24, 126
Palazzo Barberini 130, 131
Palazzo della Città Italiana 143
Palazzo Farnese 132
palm of victory (*palma*) 81
Pannini, Giovanni Paolo 136
Pantheon 9, 31, 126, 141, 142
panthers 73
passageways (*ambulacra*) 37, 109, 110, 113, 116
perfumed water dispensers 118
Pergamum amphitheatre 90
Petrarch 129
piazza 109
Pius VII, Pope 134
Pliny the Elder 22, 47
Plutarch 98, 111
podium 112, 113
Pompeii 20, 68, 80, 91, 100
   amphitheatre 20, 38–9, 41, 59, 60
populus Romanus 64
Porta Libitina 81
Priscus the gladiator 79, 100
prizes, spectator 118
Procopius 126
public executions 74–5, 77, 118
   mythical enactments 77
Pula amphitheatre 43, 44–6, 114
pulleys, cranes and winches 61
Punic Wars 66

refreshments 118
Renaissance 132–4
rhinos 6, 57, 73
Roman army 86
Roman Empire 26
   citizenship 100, 106, 107, 115
   decline of 124–6
   Eastern 29, 31, 124
   virtus 64, 118
   Western 29, 31, 124

Roman Republic 67, 97, 113
Romulus Augustulus, emperor 124

sack of Rome (AD410) 31
sack of Rome (AD455) 127
sack of Rome (AD546) 125, 126
sack of Rome (AD1084) 129
St Peter's Basilica 8, 130
Sangallo, Giuliano da 132
scenery, illusionistic 72, 79
seating 51–2, 53, 112–17
   comfort 52, 110, 115
   maenianum primum 115
   maenianum secundum 116
   ranked system 112–17
   summa cavea 39, 116–17
   summum maenianum in ligneis 52, 117
Second World War 142, 143
senators 103, 111, 112, 113, 118
Seneca 77, 118
Septimius Severus, emperor 27, 91, 98, 101
Shelley, Percy Bysshe 139
Sixtus V, Pope 134
slaves 6, 22, 51, 61, 84, 88, 117
   slave revolt 98–9
social outcasts (*infames*) 84, 100
Spartacus 42, 86–7, 93, 98–9
spectators 106–17
   crowd control 39, 41, 109–10
   dress code 107, 115
   emperor 112
   entry and evacuation 9, 109
   seating 51–2, 53, 112–17
   social profile and segregation 106, 109, 111, 113, 115
   tickets 107
   VIPs 112–13
   women 81, 110, 111, 112, 114, 117
statues 6, 45, 48, 52, 54, 61, 72, 112, 113, 126
Stendhal 6
Suetonius 26, 57, 69
Sulla 111
Symmachus 30

Tacitus 75
Taormina 37
Telemachus 30, 31, 76
Tertullian 30, 67, 77
Theatre of Marcellus 37
Theatre of Pompey 36
Theodoric 124, 125
Theodosius I, emperor 29, 30, 31, 120
Thracians 69, 78, 86–7, 90, 91, 93, 94, 95

Tiber River 25, 50
Tiberius, emperor 27
tickets 107
tigers 6, 71, 73
Titus, emperor 22, 23, 24, 25, 31, 32, 45, 48, 74, 79, 93, 100
togas 115, 116
toilets 118, 134
trainer (*lanista*) 78, 79, 84, 89–90, 97
Trajan, emperor 26, 73, 86, 106
Trajan's Column 87, 141
travertine 49, 52, 56, 126, 130, 143, 146
tunic (*chiton*) 115
Twain, Mark 6, 8

Ulpian 74
Urban VIII, Pope 131

Vandals 31, 127
Vegetius 90
Verona amphitheatre 41, 42–4, 52, 106, 111
Verus the gladiator 79, 100
Vespasian, emperor 18, 20, 22, 23, 44, 48, 50, 51
Vestal Virgins 81, 111, 112, 114
Vesuvius, Mount 38, 41
Virgil 128
Visigoths 31
Vitruvius 40, 47
voussoirs 61
vox populi 79–80

war captives 26, 66, 74, 87, 88, 89, 93
wild beast shows (*venationes*) 6, 8, 23, 26, 27, 56–7, 64, 70–3, 103, 124
   bringing animals into the arena 56–7, 58, 71, 116
   damnatio ad bestias 74–5, 77
   female hunters 23
   fights between animals 73
   hunting enactment 70–3
   scale of slaughter 6, 73
   trapping and transporting animals 71, 73, 125–6
Wittel, Caspar van 139
women
   gladiators 27, 97–8
   hunters 23
   musicians 69
   spectators 81, 110, 111, 112, 114, 117
   Vestal Virgins 81, 111, 112, 114
Wood, John (Elder and Younger) 137